THE A

Prais

It was only a matter of time before a clever publisher realized that there is an audience for whom *Exile on Main Street* or *Electric Ladyland* are as significant and worthy of study as *The Catcher in the Rye* or *Middlemarch* . . . The series . . . is freewheeling and eclectic, ranging from minute rock-geek analysis to idiosyncratic personal celebration
—*The New York Times Book Review*

Ideal for the rock geek who thinks liner notes just aren't enough—*Rolling Stone*

One of the coolest publishing imprints on the planet—*Bookslut*

These are for the insane collectors out there who appreciate fantastic design, well-executed thinking, and things that make your house look cool. Each volume in this series takes a seminal album and breaks it down in startling minutiae. We love these. We are huge nerds—*Vice*

A brilliant series . . . each one a work of real love—*NME* (UK)

Passionate, obsessive, and smart—*Nylon*

Religious tracts for the rock 'n' roll faithful—*Boldtype*

[A] consistently excellent series—*Uncut* (UK)

We . . . aren't naive enough to think that we're your only source for reading about music (but if we had our way . . . watch out). For those of you who really like to know everything there is to know about an album, you'd do well to check out Bloomsbury's "33 1/3" series of books—*Pitchfork*

For reviews of individual titles in the series, please visit our blog at 333sound.com and our website at http://www.bloomsbury.com/musican dsoundstudies Follow us on Twitter: @333books Like us on Facebook: https://www.facebook.com/33.3books

For a complete list of books in this series, see the back of this book.

Forthcoming in the series:

and many more . . .

The ArchAndroid

Alyssa Favreau

BLOOMSBURY ACADEMIC
NEW YORK · LONDON · OXFORD · NEW DELHI · SYDNEY

BLOOMSBURY ACADEMIC
Bloomsbury Publishing Inc
1385 Broadway, New York, NY 10018, USA
50 Bedford Square, London, WC1B 3DP, UK
29 Earlsfort Terrace, Dublin 2, Ireland

BLOOMSBURY, BLOOMSBURY ACADEMIC and the Diana logo are
trademarks of Bloomsbury Publishing Plc
First published in the United States of America 2021

Library of Congress Cataloging-in-Publication Data
Names: Favreau, Alyssa, author.
Title: Janelle Monáe's The ArchAndroid / Alyssa Favreau.
Description: New York : Bloomsbury Academic, 2021. | Series: 33 1/3 |
Includes bibliographical references. | Summary: "Monáe's full-length
debut, The ArchAndroid, is a science fiction concept album that tells
the story of the android Cindi Mayweather, a citizen of 28th century
Metropolis who is on the run from the authorities for daring to love a
human. As she fights for survival, Cindi realizes that she is in fact
the prophesied ArchAndroid, a robot messiah meant to liberate the masses
and lead them toward a wonderland where all can be free. This book takes
into account the literary merit of Monáe's astounding multimedia body
of work, the political relevance of the science fictional themes and

aesthetics she explores, and her role as an Atlanta-based pop cultural juggernaut. The exploration of the lavish world building present in Cindi's story, and the many literary, cinematic, and musical influences brought together to create it, will blend with a history of Monáe's move to Atlanta, her signing with Bad Boy Records, and the trials of developing of a full-length concept album in an industry overwhelmingly devoted to the production of marketable singles. The stories of Cindi and Janelle are inextricably entwined, each making the other more compelling, fantastical, and deeply felt"–Provided by publisher.

Identifiers: LCCN 2021013876 (print) | LCCN 2021013877 (ebook) | ISBN 9781501355707 (paperback) | ISBN 9781501355714 (pdf) | ISBN 9781501355721 (epub) | ISBN 9781501355738

Subjects: LCSH: Monáe, Janelle. ArchAndroid. | Science fiction in music. | Afrofuturism.

Classification: LCC ML420.M5582 F38 2021 (print) | LCC ML420.M5582 (ebook) | DDC 782.42164092–dc23

LC record available at https://lccn.loc.gov/2021013876

LC ebook record available at https://lccn.loc.gov/2021013877

ISBN: PB: 978-1-5013-5570-7
ePDF: 978-1-5013-5571-4
eBook: 978-1-5013-5572-1

Series: 33 1/3

Typeset by Deanta Global Publishing Services, Chennai, India
Printed and bound in the United States of America

To find out more about our authors and books visit www.bloomsbury.com and sign up for our newsletters.

To Cindi

Contents

Dance or Die
An Introduction

Change, when it comes, cracks everything open.
—*Dorothy Allison*[1]

On the evening of July 20, 2018, talk-show host Stephen Colbert momentarily cedes his coveted desk to another voice, and from behind a chorus of singers appears Janelle Monáe. Five-foot tall, with a bright tartan blazer and long braid whipping behind her, the singer is electric, quickly abandoning her seated, news-anchor position in favor of a microphone at the head of a checkerboard dance floor. Her message, as she sings "Americans," the final track off her 2018 album *Dirty Computer*, transcends regularly scheduled programming.

To the viewers of what is arguably the most-watched late-night network show, in an increasingly discouraging political climate, she is singing of hope, of love, and of an American identity owned and lived in not in spite of her womanhood, her Blackness, her queerness but *because* of it. It is Monáe's turn to "play god" and "defend [her] land," eschewing so-called traditional Americana in favor of a vision in which women receive equal pay for equal work, same-gender-loving people can be who they are, and Black people can return home safe from an encounter with the police. Fronted by trans actress Mj Rodriguez, the dancers are diverse in their gender presentation and beautiful in their lack of choreography, backing Monáe as she espouses a view of American identity that allows for messiness, multiplicity, and freedom. They are the "fallen angels" that nevertheless love their country enough to raise fists and bend knees. They are ready for a tough fight, but sure that victory will soon be at hand. Monáe, unabashedly happy and hopeful, inspires this confidence. It's easy to believe her, easy to believe, like the penultimate lyric proclaims, that it's going to be Monáe's America before it's all over.

For an artist who until so recently remained concealed behind a specific, manufactured persona, this outpouring of unrestrained and politically relevant emotion is nearly unheard of. For years Monáe had avoided questions about her personal life, only coming out as a pansexual "free-ass motherfucker" in a candid *Rolling Stone* cover story ahead of *Dirty Computer*'s release. It was a stark contrast to previous media appearances, where for years the only person available to the public was Monáe's futuristic pop android Cindi Mayweather.

Residing in twenty-eighth-century Metropolis, far from the America that Monáe proudly claims as her own on *Colbert*, Cindi acts as the star of and mouthpiece for Monáe's earlier conceptual work, including the 2007 *Metropolis: The Chase Suite* EP and the albums *The Archandroid* (2010) and *Electric Lady* (2013). By inhabiting Cindi Mayweather, Monáe is able to exist simultaneously as twenty-first-century pop royalty and as the legendary prototype android of that far future.

It is this Monáe to whom I am first introduced. And if her dropping *Dirty Computer* and coming out in the early months of 2018 coincided perfectly with my own queerness becoming considerably more tangible to me, it's significant that her first full-length album, *The ArchAndroid*, was released at precisely the moment when I was beginning to better understand myself. I was beginning to know that, just maybe, there was much more to me than met the eye, that I was capable of love in so many more ways than I ever could have anticipated. I may not share all of Monáe's identities, but in this way at least, my connection to her has always been strong.

My introduction to Monáe was, like many, through the infectious "Tightrope," the debut single off of *The ArchAndroid*. From those first moments, with her inimitable tuxedo, pompadour style, and molten, forceful stage presence, Monáe seemed like the second coming of James Brown, a magnetic personality I couldn't help but keep watching. In Monáe's fantastical work, where a robot sings of the critics who would see her fail and of her intention to continue to dance along a tightrope far above them, I was able to find my own nascent queerness—still a formless, unsure thing, obscured behind protective layers.

At the age of twenty, there was so much I still did not know. I hadn't even had my heart broken yet. There was a boyfriend I loved very much, despite other feelings I was still years away from fully embracing. I was captivated by this android who was androgynous but in love with someone named Anthony, who pushed the boundaries of what was appropriate and allowed in her world but who didn't push me too far out of my comfort zone. Whose metaphorical significance I instinctively understood even if I could not yet articulate it, even if I was not yet ready to articulate it. Something in Cindi Mayweather spoke to my queerness, which would come to light very soon, and to fruition many years later. For the moment, *The ArchAndroid* was the soundtrack of moving across the country from my home, of making a new home, of falling in love and learning what love was, of a university degree I hated, and of the tentative first steps into a more creative life. I carried the album with me from one apartment to the next, from career to career, from one future to a very different one.

* * *

The story of *The ArchAndroid* is part of a much grander tale, a saga that begins in the earliest days of Monáe's career and stretches up until the more personal *Dirty Computer*. The liner notes of *Metropolis*, Monáe's debut EP, offer some introductory context:

> Five World Wars have decimated the earth. To escape from the ecological destruction, mankind has banded together to create one last great city named Metropolis. Under the rule of the evil Wolfmasters, the city becomes a decadent wonderland known for its partying robo-

zillionaires, riotous ethnic, race and class conflicts and petty holocausts. But zillions come to Metropolis hoping for a better life. . . . Because if you can make it in Metropolis, you can make it anywhere.

In this world appears Cindi Mayweather, android number 57821 from the Alpha Platinum 9000 line. A synthetic being programmed with the rare rock-star proficiency package and a working soul, Cindi is a famous cybersoul singer who still must obey the rules that govern android-kind: she is forbidden to love, and most importantly must never love a human. Rules, however, are meant to be broken, and Cindi falls for the robo-zillionaire Anthony Greendown.

Cindi is immediately made an outlaw and goes on the run from the Wolfmasters, agents of a secret society called the Great Divide. This shadowy organization controls every aspect of Metropolis, using time travel to destroy freedom and love across space and time. If you have ever encountered hatred and shame, you can be sure the Great Divide has caused it. Anyone who poses a threat to their continued power is exiled, sent through time to the strange, supernatural asylum called the Palace of the Dogs.

Over the course of *The ArchAndroid*, Cindi becomes aware of her destiny, slowly realizing that she is the ArchAndroid, a cyborg messiah foretold by prophecy and fated to bring unity to Metropolis. Though it is perhaps surprising that Monáe's message of hope has its roots in so escapist a fantasy, in Cindi's world Monáe finds the space needed to explore the themes of disenfranchisement and liberation in varied, sometimes contradictory, but nevertheless cohesive ways. The legacy of science fiction writers using their stories to imagine alternative futures, better futures, is carried on in Monáe's work, a pop music expansion of an ongoing conversation.

Cindi Mayweather's path is a difficult one as she navigates the dystopia she calls home, her faith in love never wavering. As Cindi ascends from runaway to robot messiah, we can see parallels to Monáe's own rise to fame. While never purely autobiographical, in Cindi's story we find threads of Monáe's vertiginous journey from aspiring artist selling albums from the back of her car to genre-defying neosoul star paving the way for a new humanity. To say that Cindi is but a mirror would be an indefensible reduction of the scope and force of Monáe's art. But both creator and creation wield astounding power. Both are capable of bringing new imagined worlds that much closer to reality.

The ways in which Monáe deploys the android as metaphor constantly surprise—at times homage to Fritz Lang's *Metropolis*, at times an inventive new entry into the canon of Afrofuturist art. This book pays particular attention to the ways in which Monáe pulls references from the past and thrusts them into a faraway future, creating a world of limitless potential that assures her a place in a musical lineage begun by artists like Sun Ra and George Clinton. Monáe's science fictional world building, the specificity of Cindi's story as she travels through Metropolis, bolsters the universal themes of the music: the importance of love in the face of adversity, of balancing the personal and the political, of fighting for a just future.

The technofuturistic landscape of Metropolis sets the scene for Cindi's struggle, allowing a number of metaphors to take root and find power. In *The ArchAndroid* we can see the incredible role science fiction symbolism can play in the push for political change, and we can view Cindi's fight against the oppression of the Great Divide through the lens of real-world struggles against racism, misogyny, and homophobia. Metropolis is a world where the worst has happened, yes, but from this dystopian future there is much to be learned. After all, an apocalypse, from its Greek origins, is at its heart a revealing. Cindi's story is a revelation.

But all is not danger; there are pockets of safety to be found in Metropolis. One such haven is called Wondaland, a place "where dreamers meet each other,"[2] and Cindi can freely be herself. Monáe, too, finds freedom in the Wondaland Arts Society, her hybrid record company and arts collective. Her career takes flight, and does so in large part thanks to the support of Wondaland. Over the course of the next decade, she will enter the worlds of music, movies, fashion, and activism to great acclaim. Wondaland allows Monáe the creative control needed for that continued success, cementing her as an independent force in the arts, to be reckoned with for many years to come. This parallel between Cindi and Monáe, between story and storyteller, is essential.

The ArchAndroid, released by Wondaland along with Bad Boy Records, is a rich tapestry, a bricolage of places, times, and mythologies assembled with cyborg ingenuity and unforgettable beats. Produced with the support of Wondaland members, including Chuck Lightning, Nate

---

[2] "Wondaland."

"Rocket" Wonder, and Roman GianArthur, it is a complex story, a layered metaphor with a thousand different interpretations. This is only one of them. These songs will mean something singular to every single listener and are the stronger for it. My hope is for the critical examination of Janelle Monáe's music to continue for the entirety of her career, and far beyond it. For my thoughts—those I had in 2010 and the ones I have now—to be but some of many.

* * *

Only a few days before the *Colbert* performance, I'm at Monáe's Toronto concert listening to her close out the evening with "Americans." Singing to a roaring crowd and my fourth bout of tears of the evening, the concert feels like the perfect culmination of my eight-year admiration of Monáe. As I stand in the crowd, tears still streaming down my face and holding hands with a long line of concertgoers I've never met, our fists in the air, I feel a sort of frenzied catharsis. This concert is unlike any I've attended before, the climax of a relationship that has guided me through my twenties, through a time of deep transformation and self-discovery.

Listening to Monáe's music that night feels like coming full circle. It feels like a crescendo of self-assurance and pride, the thrilling completion of a hard-fought journey. Surrounded by hundreds, it's still an intimate experience, an acknowledgment that only this sort of love, for oneself, for each other, will see us through. Pausing for a moment before playing back-to-back *ArchAndroid* singles—the by-now-classic "Cold War" and "Tightrope"—Monáe says it best:

"Thank you for fighting for love. For love of humanity. . . . You realized that it is love that is going to keep us together. Nothing more. Love." In the hot press of dancing bodies, and in the wash of summer night that follows, I feel that need. The need for a sustaining, battle-ready love. For a love that is unafraid, that will fight for its own preservation.

For Monáe the personal is the political is the musical, and it always has been. One night she is screaming "I'm dirty I'm proud" to a room full of loyal concertgoers; the next she is standing in front of the American flag and proclaiming herself the true American Dream on *The Late Show with Stephen Colbert*, singing that the world and future will belong to those of us who are women, or Black, or queer. But to understand how she got here, one has to go back in time to when Monáe wasn't Monáe, but a runaway android named Cindi.

1
Tightrope

Free your mind and your ass will follow.
—*George Clinton*[1]

Janelle Monáe is not, as it would appear at first glance, a twenty-first-century singer-songwriter. If we are to take as truth the letters of Max Stellings, director of the Palace of the Dogs Asylum (provided as liner notes within *The ArchAndroid*), we must acknowledge that Janelle Monáe, patient 57821, comes to us from the year 2719. Snatched, genoraped, and de-existed—that is to say, kidnapped, her genetic code auctioned off illegally, and sent back in time—Monáe's cloned organic compounds also exist in that far-off future as the famous android Cindi Mayweather.

Residing in Metropolis, a city where, according to Stellings, "elves and dwarves, humans and androids, clones and aliens" can be found, Cindi is a paradox. Celebrated performer

---

[1] *Free Your Mind . . . and Your Ass Will Follow*, by Funkadelic. Used with permission from Bridgeport Music Inc.

but synthetic commodity, manufactured for service but so capable of love, she is at once desired and disposable, object and subject, slave and liberator. With Janelle Monáe exiled into the past, Cindi is on her own, locked in a world where "hearts of hatred rule the land" and "love is left aside."[2] Destined to become the ArchAndroid, she will have to learn to navigate a world that is wholly hostile to her, and learn the power she wields as the leader of a revolution.

Of course, we have met Cindi before. In the song "Metropolis," from Monáe's self-released 2003 demo *The Audition*, we know her as a downtrodden server living on the "wired side of town." In the EP *Metropolis: The Chase Suite*, Cindi becomes a star singer, falls in love with a human named Anthony Greendown, and is on the run from Droid Control. Her freedom is precarious, with the authorities and a slew of bounty hunters hot on her trail.

In *The ArchAndroid*, an album that encompasses suites II and III, Cindi is still in hiding, trying to stay safe, and contemplating her role in the android liberation. As the sweeping orchestral strains of the opening "Suite II Overture" give way to the relentless beat of "Dance or Die," she tells us in tense, staccato rap that "Some will pull the gun because they want to be stars / Snatching up your life into the blink of an eye." The music is low and anxious, unwilling to let the listener breathe easy as it pushes forward with unrelenting momentum. The tempo fits the situation. For all but its most elite citizens, Metropolis is a harsh world, where "war is in

---

[2] "Locked Inside."

the street and it's an eye for an eye" and the limited choices one is faced with are to "run on for your life or you can dance you can die."

But for all the danger with which Cindi is faced, it cannot keep her attention for long. She is madly, deeply, intoxicatingly in love, and as the music shifts into "Faster," the tone changes. Though the tempo remains urgent—Cindi's heart continuing to beat "like a kick drum"—the music becomes lighter, relying less on a heavy bass line, record scratches and a brightened electric guitar frenetic as Cindi addresses her lover: "You, since that magic day, we've been like magnets in a play." It's a wild, star-crossed love, one that Cindi knows logically she should run from, though she finds herself instead heading straight into the sun, melted wings be damned. Anthony Greendown has cost her everything, is for all intents and purposes her "kryptonite," and yet Cindi is caught up in an inescapable passion, wailing, "my heart beats, it beats for you and only you."

Throughout this second suite, Cindi's exploration of what it might mean, exactly, to be the ArchAndroid is continuously punctuated by these feelings. The ballad "Sir Greendown"—so reminiscent of Audrey Hepburn's "Moon River" in its dreaminess—sits between "Locked Inside" and "Cold War," songs that most explicitly deal with the class politics and robot disenfranchisement of Metropolis. But it is in the last three songs of suite II—"Oh, Maker," "Come Alive (The War of the Roses)," and "Mushrooms & Roses"—that Cindi begins to reconcile her need for love with her duty. She first asks of the unknown being who created her, "Oh, Maker, tell me did you know / This love would burn so yellow?"—wondering, perhaps, whether her capacity for love was purposely programmed into her. The aggressive rock of "Come Alive" then takes over, with Cindi letting go and proclaiming her need for release, for pleasure, for "dancing in the dungeon every Monday night." It's a hoarse, screeching sexual awakening that rips through the album, setting up then giving way to the much mellower romantic psychedelia of "Mushrooms & Roses." With Cindi, we have now arrived in "the place to be," where "all the lonely droids and lovers have their wildest dreams." In Metropolis we are all "virgins to the joys of loving without fear," and this is perhaps the exact power Cindi will bring to the role of the ArchAndroid: the ability to meet persecution with unabashed joy and a love that transcends expectation and shame.

In her work *Volatile Bodies*, feminist scholar Elizabeth Grosz writes of a desire that need not be seen as a lack, as something missing that is yearned for. Desire can, instead, be affirmative, be "what produces, what connects, what makes machinic alliances." It is this active, creative desire that fuels the machine known as Cindi, who uses the bridge of "Locked Inside" as an invocation: "I can make a change / I can start a fire / Lord make me love again / Fill me with desire"—a repeating lyric that ends with "Lord, thank you for desire." Cindi's love, far from the distraction it is presented as in "Faster," gives her the strength necessary to become the ArchAndroid. Desire will provide her with a message that will spread to the farthest reaches of Metropolis, for as Grosz writes, "desire does not take for itself a particular object whose attainment it requires; rather, it aims at nothing above its own proliferation or self-expansion." As Cindi's love grows, infiltrating the minds and hearts of humans and androids alike, Metropolis cannot help but change.

"Suite III Overture" begins as a reprise of "Mushrooms & Roses" and "Sir Greendown" enriched with piano, strings, and choir, a waltz in which Cindi urges us to follow in her footsteps and make our way to Wondaland. We are all "lost inside a lonely world where lovers pay the price," and much of suite III features an array of love songs proclaiming the liberatory possibilities of desire ("I am so inspired / You touched my wires / My supernova shining bright" from "Wondaland," as an example). Love and desire, as Cindi feels them, act as salvation and extend far beyond a single object of affection. In fact, "Mushrooms & Roses" confirms that Cindi has loved at least once before, a "regular" with "long, gray hair, beautiful smile, and rosy cheeks." Her name is Blueberry Mary and she's crazy about Cindi ("she's wild man, she's wild!"). Cindi's desire is thus explicitly queer, both in her subversive android/human love for Anthony Greendown and in terms of gender.

Arguably the earliest hint of Monáe's own sexual identity in her work, Blueberry Mary will be referenced again as "Mary" in the single "Q.U.E.E.N." from the 2013 *Electric Lady*, and as "Mary Apple 53" in the *Dirty Computer* emotion picture in 2018. A real-world example of why Cindi's interspecies love is so transgressive, mentions of Mary situate listeners in politics that are far from science fictional, grounding and empowering Monáe's metaphor. In *Cruising Utopia*, queer theorist José Esteban Muñoz discusses queerness as a concept that goes far beyond same-gender attraction, acting rather as a "rejection of a here and now and an insistence on potentiality and concrete possibility for another world." The queerness of Cindi's love, her subversion of the expectations placed upon her as a second-class citizen of Metropolis, is precisely what is needed to enact change. In loving freely, Cindi reimagines an entirely new world, and Muñoz, linking queer fantasy to utopian longing, writes of both together becoming "contributing conditions of possibility for political transformation." He urges us to "dream and enact new and better pleasures, other ways of being in the world, and ultimately new worlds" in much the same way as Cindi does when she sings "There's a world inside where dreams meet each other / Once you go it's hard to come back."[3] Queerness, Muñoz continues, is a "longing that propels us onward, beyond romances of the negative and toiling of the present. Queerness is that thing that lets us feel that this world is not enough, that indeed something is missing."

Cindi's desire, and her desire to love free of stigma, throws into sharp relief the limitations of Metropolis, and indeed our own world, all the while offering a glimpse of something else, something freer and more beautiful. Queerness, according to Muñoz, "is an invitation to desire differently, to desire more, to desire better"; queered desire *makes* Cindi the ArchAndroid, the messiah capable of making imagined worlds a reality. Though the end goal must be for us all to feel like ArchAndroids in our own lives, for the moment it is a power that is Cindi's alone, as Anthony in particular realizes in "57821": "Sir Greendown told his dear Cindi . . .

[3] "Wondaland."

I saved you so you'd save the world / 'Cause you're the only one." When Max Stellings—asylum director and potential convert—asks, "If the ArchAndroid does exist . . . can she truly save us?," the answer seems quite obvious.

And what of Cindi's unwilling progenitor exiled in our time, left in a world so far from her own? For that, we'll have to leave our twenty-eighth-century Oz, and make our way instead to Kansas, to meet a dreamer called not Dorothy but Janelle.

*　*　*

Born December 1, 1985, in Kansas City to a large Baptist family, Janelle Monáe Robinson grew up in Wyandotte County, one of the poorest in the city. Her mother was employed as a janitor while her stepfather worked at the post office and father drove a garbage truck. From a young age she contributed to the family's bills, using money won at talent competitions. Speaking to the *Chicago Tribune* in 2010, Monáe attributes her leadership skills to this early role as provider: "I had to be the rock in my family for a very long time," she says. "I always felt my duty was to help and guide."

But Monáe was nurtured in turn, her early love for music and theater encouraged. In addition to her talent show experiences—where her cover of "The Miseducation of Lauryn Hill" secured her a win three years in a row—Monáe took part in school theater productions and wrote her own musicals at the Coterie Theatre's Young Playwrights' Round Table. (An early musical, in an homage to Stevie Wonder's *Journey through "The Secret Life of Plants,"* featured a boy and girl falling in love with a plant.) Though money was tight, Monáe's mother would buy her talent show outfits. Her great-grandmothers played organ in church and taught piano.

In this supportive and musically rich environment, Monáe thrived. "It was a time when I felt most free, on stage," she would go one to tell Terry Gross on the *Fresh Air* podcast in 2009. And she made the most of that time performing, even getting kicked out of church as a young child for singing Michael Jackson's "Beat It" during the sermon. "She was always singing songs," says Monáe's mother, Janet Hawthorne. "It was uncontrollable."[4] In a Baptist church, music precedes the sermon, so that the congregation is able to "get the Holy Spirit in the music and be ready for church," Hawthorne says. But it was the music, instead, "where Janelle was ready," and when it's the music that feeds your soul, the sermon cannot help but feel like an anticlimax.

After high school, Monáe auditioned for the American Musical and Dramatic Academy (AMDA) in New York City—the only school she applied to. Seeing the academy as a golden ticket opportunity, Monáe auditioned with the song "In My Own Little Corner" from Rodgers and Hammerstein's *Cinderella*, a song she felt a strong emotional connection to after portraying the lead role in a school production. "My life really depended on that moment," she would tell Gross, and it's easy to imagine Monáe, poised to step into the next stage of her career, bringing life to a song that details the liberatory power of imagination. In her "own little corner in [her] own

---

[4] Westenberg, Emma. "Janelle Monáe—A Revolution of Love (Artist Spotlight Stories)," YouTube Music, 2018.

little chair" in Kansas City, Monáe too was dreaming of bigger things.

Despite the stalwart presence of her mother, grandmother, and aunts who, as Monáe would later write in a website bio, "to this day are some of the most powerful beings on the planet," Monáe's home life was turbulent, her childhood marked by her father's prison stints and twenty-one-year battle with addiction. A musical man himself (Monáe believes he could have had a record deal if he hadn't struggled with his addiction), Michael Robinson Summers coming in and out of his young daughter's life had a profound impact on her. "At an early age I was exposed to those around me who had gone to really dark places in their lives because of drugs," says Monáe,[5] though this only strengthened her resolve to leave and make something of herself. "I realized that I could go away and show that just because you come from a small little town in Kansas . . . You definitely have a choice."[6] In the song "In My Own Little Corner," that yearning is palpable, and singing it for an audition would prove prescient. Monáe would indeed be able to "fly anywhere" and have the world "open its arms." She was accepted to AMDA on scholarship, and *Cinderella*'s sweeping fairytale strings would reappear much later on in her own music.

Now in New York, Monáe shared a room with an older cousin who worked nights, working as a maid herself. She needed to make ends meet, though her congregation had

---

[5] "Janelle Monae's Funky Otherworldly Sounds," *Fresh Air*, 2009.
[6] "Janelle Monae: Dreaming in Science Fiction," *All Things Considered*, 2010.

taken up a collection and supplied some funds. When Monáe wasn't in class—as the only Black woman in attendance—she spent her time in libraries reading plays. But Monáe quickly felt stifled by the environment: "I felt like that was a home," she told the *Guardian* in 2010. "But I wanted to write my own musicals. I didn't want to have to live vicariously through a character that had been played thousands of times—in a line with everybody wanting to play the same person." After only a year and a half, she left AMDA, heading instead for Atlanta.

Atlanta in the 2000s thrived with a vibrant, heady mix of genres and talent that continues to this day. Writing in 2009, the *New York Times* deemed the city "hip-hop's center of gravity," and for Monáe that pull was undeniable. "Something in my heart told me to move to Atlanta," she explained in a 2010 appearance on *The Mo'Nique Show*. "Nothing special, just following my inner compass." That gut feeling would lead her to community college, a job at Office Depot, and a boarding house of six. Monáe began writing her own songs, performing them in dorm rooms, school events, and on the steps of the Robert W. Woodruff Library. She sold copies of *The Audition* out of her boarding house and the trunk of her Mitsubishi Galant, updating her MySpace page with new music during quiet moments at work (the kind of unauthorized computer use that would end up getting her fired).

A few years before, at the nearby Morehouse College, student Charles Joseph II, later known as Chuck Lightning, had established the Dark Tower Project. A Harlem Renaissance-inspired arts collective and events series, Dark Tower acted as a salon, bringing in guests like The Roots and musician, writer, and critic Greg Tate. Mikael Moore, another Morehouse student and Dark Tower member, had seen Monáe perform with her guitar on the library steps and invited her to one of Dark Tower's performance nights. It was there that Monáe met both Lightning and Nathaniel Irvin III, later known as Nate "Rocket" Wonder. "My eyes locked with Chuck's and Nate's," she would later tell the *Los Angeles Times*. "It was a weird energy, not in a negative way. Not in an 'I wanna date you' kind of way, but as in, 'I want to work with you.'"[7] A self-described "Matrix moment,"[8] this chance encounter would indeed lead to the trio working together, with Lightning and Wonder as core components of all of Monáe's subsequent music. Moore, for his part, would later become Monáe's longtime manager. "There was something about them having these big ideas," said Monáe in a *Pitchfork* profile. "I'd never met [B]lack people who were so serious and so creative, people who wanted to start a revolution and redefine music." Speaking to the *Guardian*: "It was almost like we were meant to be on the same team. We wanted to create a different blueprint."

Together, Monáe, Lightning, and Wonder would go on to form the Wondaland Arts Society, a creative collective through which they could release music independently. Atlanta proved to be the perfect place for that work, a place where, according to Monáe, "a whole lot of progressive young people, people like myself, are just trying to create something special, create something magical, create community, create

[7] Powers, Ann. "Janelle Monae in Wondaland," *Los Angeles Times*, 2010.

[8] Lynskey, Dorian. "Janelle Monáe: Sister from Another Planet," *Guardian*, 2010.

unity through art."[9] And Atlanta would continue to provide for Monáe in the form of Outkast's Antwan "Big Boi" Patton, one half of one of the city's biggest success stories. Big Boi first spotted Monáe at an open mic night singing Roberta Flack's "Killing Me Softly." Impressed, he quickly included her song "Lettin' Go" (written about Monáe's firing from Office Depot) on his 2005 *Got Purp? Vol. II* compilation album, before inviting her to be on Outkast's upcoming album *Idlewild*. "He was one of the first artists to really embrace the music that we were creating out of the Wondaland Arts Society," says Monáe,[10] and his reach would extend much farther.

Big Boi spoke about Monáe to titanic rapper/producer/ record executive Sean Combs, who then found, and loved, *Metropolis*'s "Many Moons" on MySpace. Monáe had already produced the EP independently, burned by too many meetings with record label executives eager to change everything from her music to her wardrobe—at the time, comprised exclusively of tuxedos, a pompadour, and saddle shoes, a James Brownesque performer's uniform worn to honor Monáe's blue-collar roots. "I had to make sure that I stood up for the things that I believed in," she says. "The right to wear a tuxedo, the right to have a concept album. When you feel like your rights are being taken away from you, you start to rebel—which has really worked for my career."[11]

[9] Westenberg.

[10] "Getting to Know Janelle Monae: Comments on Getting Fired, Big Boi & Diddy," *Dropout UK*, 2010.

[11] Mossman, Kate. "Janelle Monáe: 'I'm a Time Traveller. I Have Been to Lots of Different Places," *Guardian*, 2013.

Already determined to make a go of it without corporate help, Combs's call came at an ideal moment for Monáe: She had no need to compromise, and nothing to lose. She would hear his offer only if he saw her perform beforehand, and Combs dutifully stopped filming his show *Making the Band* in order to fly to Atlanta. "It was important to know if he was serious," says Monáe, "that he was going to appreciate me and not try to change my live show or my music."[12] Combs came, saw, and set up a meeting for the following day.

The deal was this: Combs's Bad Boy Records would offer resources and promotion, but would have no creative control over Monáe and her work. It would be a notable departure for someone known for closely (micro-)managing talent—a trait on full display in the show he took time off from to see Monáe. But in Monáe, Combs saw a fully realized artist, telling the *New York Times Magazine*, "It was immediate. I just knew she was going to be important to music and culture. It was the same sort of feeling I had when I first heard Biggie or Mary J. Blige, and I wanted to help introduce this artist to the world." Monáe signed with Bad Boy and Atlantic Records in 2008, reissuing an expanded and now Grammy-nominated *Metropolis: The Chase Suite*.

The partnership was exactly what the Wondaland team needed. According to Chuck Lightning, Combs protected them, acting as a "guardian of what we wanted to do. He was absolutely perfect. He saw the vision first." As Monáe

[12] Wortham, Jenna. "How Janelle Monáe Found Her Voice," *New York Times Magazine*, 2018.

would later tell *SPIN*, "creative independence is my air, it is my water." With Combs's more laissez-faire attitude—never editing, only pushing—Monáe had the platform needed to embark on a full-length album. It would be a concept piece, like *Metropolis*, about a runaway android destined for greater things. Now with the resources of both Bad Boy and Atlantic at her disposal, the scene was set. *The ArchAndroid* could be brought to life, along with a first single featuring a familiar mentor: Big Boi himself.

*   *   *

"Tightrope" explodes. From its first moments, the percussive blast is enough to send even the most stubborn heads bobbing. As Big Boi introduces us to Monáe and his own alter ego Sir Lucious Left Foot, a wail rings out, accompanying a high-tempo promise to take the listener's pain away. As the dry, infectious bass line takes over, Monáe extolls the virtues of balance, of knowing one's worth when doubted, and staying centered when elevated to great heights.

"Tightrope was written for the people," Monáe would say during her appearance on *The Mo'Nique Show*. Conceptualized as "a tutorial on how to stay sane in this world," the song was made for the oppressed, for people held back from being singular. "I wanted to give them a song where they can get funky, have that inner confidence come out, and fight off any haterism that may be coming their way." The song's production works remarkably well to get that message across. As Monáe cycles from mellow spoken word to Michael Jackson-style screaming, her voice levels stay even, sounding intimately close.[13] Though the reverb on the song's horns, strings, and backing vocals creates a large sense of scale, amid this vast sonic world Monáe is right there, delivering a personal message to each individual listener. Some might call her a sinner, and some might call her a winner, but it has no effect on her, she's just there "callin' you to dinner."

It was a strong first message for a song that would introduce Monáe to a much wider audience, a message that spoke to the singer's wisdom and desire for longevity. As much as "Tightrope" is a pep talk, it also functions as a warning, cautioning to not let success overshadow artistry, to strive for more than a flash in the pan. In that respect, Big Boi's presence on the track feels important. "Big Boi's been in the industry for a very long time," says Monáe, again on *The Mo'Nique Show*. "It was right for him to get on and speak about his perspective and how he deals with the highs and lows of the industry and life." The song never loses its fun, and Big Boi's singsong delivery refuses to take the endeavor too seriously, but his authority is nevertheless apparent.

Having such an established guest artist is also strategic, placing Monáe firmly within a musical tradition. Between the funk bass line, tuxedoed dancing, and melodies reminiscent of "Get Up (I Feel Like Being a) Sex Machine," the allusion to James Brown is clear. With the additional presence (and

---

[13] There's truth to that intimacy: The Happy Birthdays at the end of the song, sung in the strings' melody, were originally sung over the phone to Wondaland MC, DJ, and host George 2.0, a quick late-night break in the recording session that made it into the final product.

endorsement) of Big Boi, Monáe is being set up as the next step in an ongoing legacy, a genre-hopping continuation of Black American music paying tribute to the past but focused squarely on the future.

"Tightrope" is the song that has the least explicit relationship to the Cindi Mayweather story, and that too seems deliberate. Better to ease an audience into the science fictional world of Metropolis, rather than to throw them headfirst into the complex lore of the ArchAndroid and the Great Divide. According to Lightning, in an interview included with *The ArchAndroid*'s iTunes LP deluxe edition,

> We wanted it to be more of a dance song. We're not going to sacrifice the jam just to tell about how Cindi did this or Anthony's going through that. . . . This is a song where we could have learned something about robo-zillionaires and what they meant, but we decided to pull back and learn more about what it means to be one person walking for freedom and trying to stay balanced. Which is an ArchAndroid thing.

In a time where singles were still expected to be an album's calling card and an advertisement to encourage album purchases, the captivating and accessible "Tightrope" seemed like a sure thing. As Lightning told me, it all came down to one fundamental question: "What songs feel reactive? What songs make you lean forward towards the speakers and maybe bob your head? Make your body react in a reptilian, lizard brain way?" With the team overjoyed at the prospect of having an album, of getting their vision out in the world, Lightning says the reasoning for foregrounding "Tightrope" was very much: "We need some songs that people can get excited about, and listen to, and say, 'Oh I want to hear this whole thing.' I think 'Tightrope' stood out to everybody as a record that sold what we were doing on the funk side." The maneuver paid off, earning the song a Grammy nomination for Best Urban/Alternative Performance, and eighth place on *Rolling Stone*'s Best Songs of 2010 list. But for those fans who did want more of Cindi's story, "Tightrope" could still deliver.

All we see at the start of the "Tightrope" video is a black screen, white text introducing the Palace of the Dogs Asylum, where "dancing has long been forbidden for its subversive effects on the residents and its tendency to lead to illegal magical practices." As the eerie strains of "Cold War (Wondamix)" are replaced by the song proper, a stern nurse rolls a cart down a dim hallway, her pills spilling out of small cups, soon to subdue the inmates. But despite these hostile surroundings, from Cindi's—or perhaps Monáe's—first moments on screen she is already a rule breaker, singing and dancing with a group of dancers picked specifically for their Memphis-based style of dance called Jookin. The group, including renowned street dancer Lil Buck in his first music video role, seems to float its way down the hallway, feet slaloming as if on skates.

The result does indeed feel magical, an effect that director Wendy Morgan says was necessary to bring life to the asylum. "The Palace of the Dogs is Institution," she told me, "it's a place where people were trying to control creative people, stop them, bog them down with drugs to stop them from spreading their ideas and their revolution. Everything that art is." The Palace exists in a different reality, an "otherworldly, timeless place where someone from the future would crisscross with someone from the past," according to Morgan. Time travel is thus weaponized, used to hold thinkers and artists hostage, away from their own times and the places where they could make a difference. But the asylum perhaps offers an opportunity as well: a meeting place in which to foster alliances between great imaginative minds, like those of author and perennial Wondaland inspiration Octavia E. Butler, and Afrofuturist jazz composer Sun Ra.

Allusions to Sun Ra, and particularly his film *Space Is the Place*, are lurking just around the corner. The 1974 film opens on an unearthly garden through which Ra calmly walks, telling the story of his attempts to create a colony away from the Earth and its sounds of "guns, anger, and frustration." The musician desires to create a place with different music, different vibrations, where Black people could "see what they can do with a planet all their own without any white people there." As Ra lays out this plan, he is followed by a cloaked figure with a mirrored face, the same as the figures that haunt the halls of the Palace of the Dogs.

These figures—asylum guards, physical manifestations of the Great Divide—offer an intriguing reading: that those with power will always need the powerless against whom to compare themselves, will always need an Other to delineate the boundaries of the Self. But the cloaked figures also imply that liberation is possible when the oppressed are allowed to be more than the mere reflection of their oppressors. For Sun Ra, creating a space apart, a new world in which to cultivate Black excellence, is key. Similarly, for Cindi true power will

Figure 1 The mirror faced figure from *Space Is the Place* (© 1973 Jim Newman).

only come when she transcends the role of the android, that mass-produced human simulacrum bound to serve, embodying her fullest potential as the ArchAndroid.

Sun Ra uses time travel and music to recruit volunteers to his resettlement program, and these tools—usually so tightly

Figure 2 The same mirror-faces in the "Tightrope" music video (© 2010 WMG/Bad Boy Records, LLC).

controlled by the Great Divide—are very much at Cindi's disposal as well. "We wanted to show that Janelle had the ability to escape, and had this higher power," says Morgan, "like this was just a chapter." As Monáe, or Cindi, dances away from the slowly advancing mirrored figures, she passes through walls, unhindered by the obstacles of the asylum. The figures pursue her, and she obediently returns, but the tone remains light. Cindi, or Monáe, knows that she has the power to leave but acknowledges that the time is not yet right. "The people held in the Palace of the Dogs, including Janelle Monáe, including Octavia Butler, were probably going to have to do something together to rise against," says Morgan. Just as Sun Ra declares that we are to "consider time officially ended," that his work will take place "on the other side of time," the out-of-time Palace of the Dogs can act as resource rather than prison. The presence of this budding ArchAndroid will undoubtedly have consequences as she continues to learn and grow, to make alliances and find kindred spirits. There is still much to be done, and the connections still to be made harken back to the power of the ArchAndroid, the power to find love even in those places where it seems absent. With a final lingering, soulful glance directly at the camera, Monáe, or Cindi, assures us that she will return, and that anything can be conquered with dancing and time travel and love.

*　*　*

Discussing the lack of love found in *our* world, public intellectual bell hooks writes in her work *All About Love* that it is "especially hard to speak of love when what we have to say calls attention to the fact that lovelessness is more common than love." Anguish in the face of lovelessness—of war, hunger, violence, and all the ways a lack of love manifests— is an appropriate reaction, one that can be counteracted only through knowledge of love. Love, according to hooks, may very well be the "only sane and satisfactory response to the problem of human existence," the only force capable of giving meaning and purpose to life. Audre Lorde, the Grande Dame of theorizing the erotic, builds upon the idea of love as source of meaning: "Our erotic knowledge empowers us, becomes a lens through which we scrutinize all aspects of our existence, forcing us to evaluate those aspects honestly in terms of their relative meaning within our lives."[14] Lorde's erotic is a deep sense of satisfaction and completion, one that can manifest in desire and sex, but is certainly not confined to that sphere. The erotic is a bridge between the spiritual and the political, a necessary step in demanding "for ourselves and our life-pursuits that they feel in accordance with that joy which we know ourselves to be capable of." Once one possesses knowledge of the erotic, or of hooks's love, it becomes impossible, according to Lorde, "to settle for the convenient, the shoddy, the conventionally expected . . . the merely safe."

Monáe herself often speaks of love, telling *Entertainment Tonight* during Pride 2020 that "love is the purest thing and one of the most important things that we can possess for ourselves and for others." This has been her constant refrain throughout the years, that though it is "hard for us to love . . . it's the best thing when it happens. If you look throughout history, you look throughout any movement, love had to be at the center of it. It's contagious. It's a good virus. I want to infect people with love."[15] Here the political implications of love become clear. When Monáe says that love "has the power to change the world,"[16] she means it quite literally. In his 1958 essay "An Experiment in Love," Martin Luther King Jr. writes that to "meet hate with retaliatory hate would do nothing but intensify the existence of evil in the universe." He means instead to fight with a love he terms *agape*, or "understanding, redeeming goodwill for all."

[14] "Uses of the Erotic: The Erotic as Power."

[15] Westenberg.

[16] Ibid.

Although King is often erroneously remembered by white America as somewhat toothless, his discursive contributions indefensibly whitewashed, his *agape* is anything but passive. "It would be nonsense to urge men to love their oppressors in an affectionate sense," he writes, continuing: "*Agape* is not a weak, passive love. It is love in action. *Agape* is love seeking to preserve and create community. It is insistence on community even when one seeks to break it. *Agape* is a willingness to go to any length to restore community."

Cindi's turn toward love, toward the liberatory potential of the ArchAndroid, is not a surrender. Her brand of emancipation may come in the form of love and pleasure—an infectious mix of Lorde's erotic, King's *agape*, and her own transgressive desire—but by embracing an ethos of love, of compassion, Cindi is entering into a political arena in which she will bear the brunt of Metropolis's violence. But much like protestors who face police brutality head-on, not as a passive ceding of power but to deliberately lay bare the force that is used against them every day, Cindi exposes herself to dismantle the oppressive forces of Metropolis. She seems prepared to meet the cruelty and dismissal of her world with a constructive, loving strength.

Over the course of *The ArchAndroid*, an album anchored by a single focused on balance, on the need to "tip on the tightrope," she will have to stay the course between her love and her revolution. She will have to remain centered, the perfectly balanced mediator, the heart of Metropolis. The responsibility is a heavy one to bear, but our ArchAndroid is perfectly qualified. Besides, this is not the first time that this story has been told.

2
Neon Gumbo

The future enters into us in order to transform
itself in us long before it happens.
—*Rainer Maria Rilke*[1]

An orchestra swells, horns bright and bombastic, heralding
the film's opening epigraph, which proclaims in all-caps
grandiloquence that "THE MEDIATOR BETWEEN
BRAIN AND HANDS MUST BE THE HEART!" The music
continues unabated, pulsed forward by kettledrums as a
glittering cityscape fades in. Tall and radiant with all the
promise of twentieth-century industry, the buildings are
seen from below, imposingly beautiful with their hundreds
of windows. Behind the towering peaks, shards of light
become first searchlights, then arced radio waves in a climax
of growth, increase, and progress.

But there is only a brief moment of rest before the score
rushes us forward, or rather downward, to where frantic,

---

[1] *Letters to a Young Poet.*

thrusting pistons, whirling cogs, and ticking clocks make all the abundance of the surface possible. The scene reaches a fever pitch with a strident call and bellowing steam, signals of a shift change. The first characters we see are uniformed workers, shuffling in lockstep as they pass through barred gates and travel even deeper below the earth's surface to the workers' city. Still in formation, seemingly unable to break free even in the off-hours, this literal underclass exits its elevator. Another shift will start soon enough.

* * *

Any look at the Cindi Mayweather saga and its influences must start with *Metropolis*. In story, aesthetic, and philosophy, Fritz Lang's 1927 German Expressionist masterpiece is the most obvious source of inspiration. A 2010 *Rolling Stone* interview makes clear that connection, reporting that the basics of Cindi's story came to life after a viewing of the silent film. "It represents what we're still going through," Monáe is quoted as saying. "It's about the battle between the haves and the have-nots." An understanding of Lang's work is necessary to even begin to parse the themes and messaging of *The ArchAndroid*. So let's take a short trip to *Metropolis*.

Written by Thea von Harbou, Lang's wife and author of the original novel on which the film was based, *Metropolis* tells the story of Freder, son of a powerful city planner. Freder lives a life of ease in Metropolis, a megacity so tall and grand that airplanes fly beneath tramways, and the skyscrapers seem to never end. Freder enjoys himself among the gardens, libraries, and stadiums that make up the Club of the Sons until, after a chance encounter, he falls in love with the poor Maria.

A spiritual leader prophesying the arrival of a Mediator, Maria believes that such a savior will soon appear to heal the rift between those who own and profit from the machines, and those who spend, and sacrifice, their lives working them. Freder leaves the Eternal Gardens and the fountains, white peacocks, and beautiful women that populate them, and goes in search of Maria only to be confronted with the abysmal working conditions on which his lifestyle relies.

Jolted out of his complacency by the exploitation he witnesses, Freder eventually attends a meeting led by Maria. She holds the crowd captive, telling a modified story of the Tower of Babel, in which the noble act of creation is twisted into something perverse when the heads that conceive of the project become alienated from the hands that enact it. In Maria's version, the tragic outcome arrives not in the form of divinely mandated multilingualism but in the very fact that "people spoke the same language, but could not understand each other." Here it is class division that halts understanding, and, as Maria repeats the film's opening declaration, she is convinced that only the peaceful reunion of the head and the hands, brought about by the heart, will heal her world. Maria and Freder meet, and she quickly identifies him as the sought-after Mediator, the heart sent to bring Metropolis back into balance.

Meanwhile, Freder's father sits in the New Tower of Babel, his center of operations, not amused by his son's newfound political fervor. He visits the inventor Rotwang, who has been working on a "Machine-Man." Rotwang may well call the robot the "man of the future," but this synthetic life form is coded decidedly female, with a sculpted metal body and blank expression. Freder's father commands Rotwang to kidnap Maria and replace her with the disguised Machine-Man, the better to discredit her, incite the workers to violence, and give him a pretext for retaliation. When the mechanized Maria is deployed, it is with a dark mouth, heavily kohled eyes, and swaying hips—weaponized femininity, the downfall of Man. She performs, driving her audience to distraction, culminating in the act's final scene: Maria as the Whore of Babylon, astride a statue of a seven-headed beast, one head for each deadly sin, and the robot mistress of them all.

Machine Maria whips the workers into a riotous frenzy, convincing them to destroy the machines they work on night and day. This causes the underground workers' city to flood and puts the lives of all the children left behind at risk. As violence grows, Freder's father remains unmoved until he realizes that he has put his own son in harm's way as well. The workers turn on Machine Maria, casting her into the fire, and together Freder and his father save the real Maria from Rotwang. The film ends with Freder physically bringing his father and the machines' foreman together, as Maria entreats, "Head and hands want to join together, but they don't have the heart to do it. . . . Oh mediator, show them the way to each other." As Gottfried Huppertz's score swells, Freder reaches for them both, a heart caring and clear-eyed enough to mediate between head and hands.

From the name of the 2007 EP to the visual similarities between *The ArchAndroid*'s album cover and the film's Heinz Schulz-Neudamm-designed poster, the Expressionist film's DNA can be found throughout. Even the decision to adorn Cindi with a skyline crown—coincidental, according to Chuck Lightning, a choice made after seeing a fashion photograph of a model wearing an Empire State Building headpiece—speaks to how deeply, even subconsciously, embedded *Metropolis* is in the imaginary of the ArchAndroid.

From the far-future megacity setting to its focus on ostensibly unassailable class divisions, the ethos of Lang's work can be felt at every step. In Cindi, we see a similar revolutionary power given to a synthetic life form, and love held up as the only method to achieve peace between ruling and underclasses. As in Lang's *Metropolis*, Cindi's story is one in which a savior is needed to heal wounds that extend deep into a city's foundation, and likely stretch back to its founding. "She's the mediator between the haves and have-notes," says Monáe in 2010 in *New York Magazine*, thereby making the link explicit. "[Cindi is] the chosen one to help restore unity and balance." And while *Metropolis* stands as a central reference point for understanding Cindi's journey, more interesting is the way in which these elements are repurposed and remixed to tell a crucially different story.

In Cindi, the stories of both Maria and Freder are combined, Monáe's android embodying at once oppressed object and savior capable of righting generational wrongs. Maria's (and Machine Maria's) narrative transformation from revolutionary leader to tool of the ruling class is reversed and expanded, with Cindi beginning life as commodity before coming into her role as the ArchAndroid, firmly the protagonist in her own story. Maria's journey from human woman to technological creation is similarly flipped,

Figure 3 1926 promotional poster for *Metropolis* by Heinz Schulz Neudamm (© The Museum of Modern Art/Licensed by SCALA/ Art Resources, NY).

with Cindi's decision to love freely an appropriation of an experience explicitly reserved for the humans of Metropolis. The choice to love brings her closer to the more organic parts of her heritage, solidifying her as a cyborg born of both human and machine.

In combining Maria's transformation with Freder's messianic destiny, the Cindi Mayweather saga joins a personal and character-driven arc to one of social and religious change. While Freder accepts his role as mediating Heart immediately and without question, Cindi struggles, unsure of her ability to shoulder such a responsibility. Despite her relatively privileged position as famous singer and prototype of the Alpha Platinum 9000 line, Cindi's sense of herself as chosen one is by no means a given. (This dynamic can best be seen in the reassuring call and response of "I wonder if I am the one" / "You're the one" in "57821.")

Rather than have her android nature be her downfall, as it does for the Machine Maria, it is ultimately what allows Cindi to bridge the divide between human and machine. Machine Maria may be electrifying, actress Brigitte Helm flinging her body in every direction as she fans the flames of discontent, but hers is a fervor that seeks to sever, not unite. When she commands the mob with frothing cries of "Let the machines starve, you fools—! Let them die—!!" "Kill them—the machines—!!" without pausing to consider that she might become the very machine to be raged against, her actions prove fatal.

Here is where *Metropolis* begins to fail Monáe. The film is perfectly willing to use the figure of the robot as merely a tool of industrial hubris, a dangerous foot soldier without agency who must be disposed of on the funeral pyre. Cindi's story, however, is much more interested in exploring the complexities, paradoxes, and potentialities of cyborg identity.

In her 1985 essay "A Cyborg Manifesto," science and technology theorist Donna Haraway writes of a concept born of the natural and the artificial, descended both from organically evolved life and from mechanical creation. This cyborg exists in the in-between of human and machine, blurring the boundary separating them through its very presence on that boundary. In contrast to the two Marias of Lang's *Metropolis*, a true cyborg can be both virtuous woman and threatening machine, able to see from multiple perspectives and unafraid of "permanently partial identities and contradictory standpoints." According to Haraway, by the late twentieth century machines had "made thoroughly ambiguous the difference between natural and artificial, mind and body, self-developing and externally designed, and many other distinctions that used to apply to organisms and machines."

The cyborg, as real-world phenomenon and as imaginative resource in the realm of science fiction, makes these distinctions obsolete. What need have we of a human-machine dichotomy when so many of us rely on cyborg technologies, from pacemakers to contact lenses? And when the most humane character in *The ArchAndroid*'s story is a robot singer fighting for her rights, insistence on the separation of the mechanical and the animal seems hopelessly out of date. "Our machines are disturbingly lively," writes Haraway, who could so easily be writing about the heart-quickening high notes of "Come Alive." We humans, by comparison, "feel frighteningly inert."

The cyborg is a being of infinite connection, skeptical of any single story or any one point of view, but needy for networks and "pleasurably tight couplings." Cindi, caught in her search for love, for community, for the chance to no longer suffer the "rare, rare blue" of living in a world so full of hate,[2] is the perfect cyborg. For only a cyborg can navigate Metropolis, understand the injustice at its core, and yet find love enough to try to save it.

In Cindi's rebellious spirit we can also see flashes of the cyborg, a marginal creature so entirely its own that it feels no loyalty to those who created it. Cyborgs, for Haraway, are illegitimate offspring "often exceedingly unfaithful to their origins." And how could they be faithful, when they represent all that is new, fluid, and ever-changing? All that exists in the gray, the middle spaces, the margins?

Throughout *The ArchAndroid* Cindi defies any attempts to pin her down, moving from song to song, genre to genre, from one feeling to another, ricocheting with gleeful abandon. In "Make the Bus," Of Montreal front man Kevin Barnes sings reproachfully, "I saw you spit on London, just like you were a Peter Pan," and what a perfect comparison it is for the freewheeling cyborg unwilling to fall in line, impish and uncontrollable in her childlike appetite for pleasure. "Come Alive," too, has such an energy, Cindi "kicking at your window and keeping you up," getting wild and refusing to be subdued.

Although the cyborg deals in desire and chaos, unthinking hedonism is not what drives it. For the cyborg is also a "world-

[2] "Oh, Maker."

changing fiction" with the power to imagine and create much-needed political change. Cyborgs are "an argument for *pleasure* in the confusion of boundaries and for *responsibility* in their construction," writes Haraway. It takes someone living on the boundaries, the outskirts of what is deemed possible, to change those boundaries and see value in the change. The cyborg's political struggle, the struggle that only the cyborg can assume, is "to see from both perspectives at once because each reveals both dominations and possibilities unimaginable from the other vantage point." And so when Cindi looks inward to both the machine and the human, the parts of her at once so sure of her love but also amazed that her emotions can "explode from gray to black then bloody wine" at all,[3] it is that very cyborg nature that shows her the way to her destiny.

Cindi's journey toward becoming the ArchAndroid is, as she says herself in "BaBopByeYa," one she makes "singing a love song and the words I wrote I wrote for two." Anthony and Cindi, human and android, have and have-not—these two natures exist side by side in all of us, and any song with the power to change the world will be, must be, sung for them both. Cindi's ultimate goal of leading "us all back to one / Indivisible sum"[4] won't be achieved by flattening the many intersecting identities alive and well within us, but by embracing them and creating space for them within her unity.

The cyborg story is one of "transgressed boundaries, potent fusions, and dangerous possibilities which progressive

[3] Ibid.
[4] "57821."

people might explore as one part of needed political work," writes Haraway. By inhabiting multiple viewpoints at once the cyborg acts as mechanism through which political transformation can be imagined, making science fiction storytellers "theorists for cyborgs," thinkers doing necessary political labor for change. For Haraway, there is no boundary between science fiction and social reality. The work the cyborg can do in one can equally be done in the other.

Outside of Metropolis, we can see that it is not Cindi alone who lives up to the cyborg moniker. Just as Haraway's cyborg gains its power from operating both as literary metaphor and as real-world phenomenon, Cindi's robot nature is mirrored and strengthened by Janelle Monáe's use of technology as an artist. Monáe's voice is modulated, made machinic, in almost all of *The ArchAndroid*'s songs. It is a technological mediation that allows her to easily, polymorphically pass between genres, but most importantly allows her to center the artificiality of her alter ego.

From the blissed out, watery vocals of "Mushrooms & Roses" to the doubled and two octaves-lower echoes in "Faster," from the robotic rapped breakdown of "Neon Valley Street," to the manipulated climax of "Come Alive" that exists just beyond what sounds properly human, examples of the more-than-human can be found throughout. Monáe's voice, Cindi's voice, is petulant in "Make the Bus" but playful in "Wondaland." The choral arrangement in the "Suite III Overture" harkens to another time, conjuring memories of the reverbed close harmonies of the Disney Chorus. "Neon Gumbo," functioning as interlude separating the confident manifesto of "Tightrope" from the more introspective "Oh,

Maker," turns out to be the closing lullaby from Monáe's previous single "Many Moons"—itself heavily modified—but played backward. Synths, phasers, and a mellotron round out the album's otherworldly sound.

"This tension between the nonhuman and human, presence and absence," writes African American studies scholar Alexander G. Weheliye, "reaches its pinnacle in the traffic between [B]lack popular music and the various recording and reproduction technologies it has been transmitted through over the course of the twentieth century." In his work "'Feenin': Posthuman Voices in Contemporary Black Popular Music," Weheliye discusses Black American music, and soul and R&B in particular, as embracing new technologies and thereby foregrounding "self-consciousness about the performative aspects of soul." There is, in Weheliye's view, a tension between the human and the posthuman in Black popular music precisely because of its roots in the *de*humanizing forces of slavery. Such a history naturally makes the category of "human" suspect, with entry a privilege not often bestowed by white America and always in danger of being rescinded. As Weheliye writes: "The human has had a very different meaning in [B]lack culture and politics than it has enjoyed in mainstream America."

That self-consciousness, the understanding of the human as a contentious category, has manifested in popular music as an ironic adoption of "non-human" technologies like the vocoder. "The vocoder effect in [B]lack popular music amplifies the human provenances of the voice," says Weheliye, "highlighting its virtual embodiment, [and yet] bolstering the 'soulfulness' of the human voice. Here, the 'human' and 'machinic' become mere electric effects that conjoin the human voice and (intelligent) machines." By purposefully embracing technologies that render the human voice less human, Weheliye argues that the effect is to bypass the label of "human" in favor of the "posthuman"—a cyborg state that refuses binary categorization.

Moreover, Weheliye does not limit himself to discussions of voice-altering technologies, adding that remixing, scratching, and sampling also serve to emphasize the virtuality of recorded music. "Acknowledging the effects of these technologies on these musical practices," he writes, "[B]lack popular musical genres make their own virtuality central to the musical texts." This is accomplished by highlighting the role of producers, rather than having them operate from the shadows. Producers, "who plug the performers into the technological apparatus, take front and center stage with the artists," writes Weheliye. "This creates a composite identity, a machine suspended between performer and producer that sounds the smooth flow between humans and machines."

Along with Chuck Lightning and Nate Wonder, Monáe does indeed sample widely: with the drums from Michael Jackson's "Rock with You" coming in swinging in the second verse of "Locked Inside"; "Suite III Overture" transitioning from whimsy to something more pensive with an interpolation of "Pure Imagination" from *Willy Wonka & the Chocolate Factory*;[5] as well as "Say You'll Go," which gently dissolves into a moment of Claude Debussy's "Clair de lune."

---

[5] More specifically, "Wonkavator/End Title (Pure Imagination)" from the 1971 film's score.

Monáe's work with Lightning and Wonder represents exactly the type of democratized artist-producer creative partnership that Weheliye examines. Though publicly Monáe stands alone as incomparable solo act, the Wondaland collective and its effect on her career have always been a principal component of her celebrity image. In the *Los Angeles Times* in 2010, Ann Powers describes the relationship between Monáe, Lightning, and Wonder as recasting "the usual top-down relationship of producer and 'diva' as something far more fluid and equal," with Monáe then adding: "We're actually androids when we work. Or cyborgs." She's not wrong; the ways in which Monáe, Lighting, and Wonder operate seem like nothing so much as a decentralized network of cyborg minds and porous boundaries, three individuals no longer separate as they take on this act of creation.

*   *   *

Monáe's approach to music making, that interplay between past and future, between looking to what has come before for inspiration and using production technologies and storytelling conventions that point to a far future, is decidedly Afrofuturist. An aesthetic and philosophy arguably begun by Sun Ra and his Arkestra in the 1950s, Afrofuturism is a lens through which to view African diaspora and extrapolate it into the future. Much of Afrofuturist art, from Parliament-Funkadelic to *Black Panther*, has as an explicit goal to bring Blackness into a technofuture, that space so often reserved for the brave white hero busily shooting aliens with lasers.

In her book *Afrofuturism*, Ytasha L. Womack describes a "liberation edict" providing a "prism for evolution." Afrofuturism is, for Womack, "imagination, hope, and the expectation for transformative change." It is the knowledge that all of diaspora culture, expression, heritage, and wisdom can, should, and will occupy a place of privilege in our futures.

Coined by Mark Dery in his 1994 work "Black to the Future: Interviews with Samuel R. Delany, Greg Tate, and Tricia Rose," the term "Afrofuturism" handily answers Dery's own questions:

> Can a community whose past has been deliberately rubbed out, and whose energies have subsequently been consumed by the search for legible traces of its history, imagine possible futures? Furthermore, isn't the unreal estate of the future already owned by the technocrats, futurologists, streamliners, and set designers—white to a man—who have engineered our collective fantasies?

Afrofuturism is then the attempt to wrest control of the future, the stories told and the possibilities imagined, away from a mainstream understanding that would see only the white and the masculine as worthy of inhabiting it—a collection of "semiotic ghosts . . . [that] still haunt the public imagination."

Though the political work of Afrofuturism is sorely needed, joy exists within as well. Happiness and freedom spring from the limitless possibilities of a future opening up, and beautiful chaos in new ideas being imagined, experimented with, allowed to flourish. When asked by Roxane Gay in a

2020 interview for *The Cut* what an Afrofuture would look like to her, Monáe unleashed the full force of that joy:

> Right now, it's Lil Uzi Vert being happy with orange locs, Erykah Badu doulaing, Octavia Butler's voice, Stacey Abrams being president and punching Trump out the Oval seat, [B]lack people getting passports and hanging out in Africa, [B]lack queer lovers holding hands while the pastor smiles, George Clinton's sunglasses in 1974, Prince's eyeliner in *Under the Cherry Moon,* [B]lack bodies walking away alive after a police stop, Tierra Whack and Ari Lennox joking on Twitter, [B]lack kings in nail polish, Lupita's performance in *Us.* It looks like an orgasm and the big bang happening while skydiving as Grace Jones smiles.

To be an Afrofuturist is to be unknowable to white supremacy. It is to escape to the outside of mainstream culture and its understandings of what the future will bring, to escape the single story told for so long. As Greg Tate says in his interview with Dery, Afrofuturism, jumping off science fiction's "basic human desire to know the unknowable," is directed "toward self-knowledge." To be Afrofuturist is to look to the past to help imagine the future, and to use the joy of an as yet unwritten future to strengthen one's connection to that past.

Much has been written about how the history of the African diaspora, precipitated as it was by slave trade and Middle Passage, can be mapped onto more (science) fictional experiences of Otherness. Dery is no exception, stating that "African Americans, in a very real sense, are the descendants of alien abductees; they inhabit a sci-fi nightmare in which unseen but no less impassable force fields of intolerance frustrate their movements." Similarly, the lineage of the robot is rooted in bondage, one that begins with Karel Čapek's 1920 play *R.U.R.: Rossum's Universal Robots*, passes by Asimov's Three Laws of Robotics, and through to the present-day ethics of *Ex Machina* and *Westworld*.

In her interview with Dery, Tricia Rose discusses hip-hop artists understanding themselves as "*already having been robots*" and adopting the robot as alter ego as a response to a preexisting condition: "namely, that they were labor for capitalism, that they had very little value as people in this society." Cindi's lineage as robot or cyborg is not only musical and artistic but political as well. The alienation of the robot is, according to Tate, "the condition of alienation that comes from being a [B]lack subject in American society . . . Black people live the estrangement that science fiction writers imagine."

If it seems strange that a phenomenon called Afro*futurism* is so concerned with establishing lineage and recapturing heritage, Tate provides the answer: "You can be backward-looking and forward-looking at the same time." Speaking specifically of hip-hop, Tate is quick to reconcile the paradox, saying, "the approach to everything in hip-hop is always with a sense of play, so that even ancestor worship is subject to irreverence." In hip-hop, and arguably Afrofuturist music more generally, "the trappings of tradition are never allowed to stand in the way of innovation and improvisation." Afrofuturism, while not a utopian paradigm—one need look no farther than the horrors of Cindi's Metropolis to establish that—is nevertheless characterized by that sense of play, the celebratory experimentation that joins together past and future, the better to understand the present. And if the Great Divide represents anything, it is the force against which Afrofuturism fights. A weaponized erasure of the past that can be combated only by bringing past and future together.

In *Cruising Utopia*, José Esteban Muñoz urges us to "vacate the here and now for a then and there," writing that attempts to reach an imagined better future must be communal and sought after together. "Individual transports are insufficient," he writes. "We need to engage in a collective temporal distortion." Afrofuturism's ability to bring together the past and future of an entire people seems the perfect method through which to achieve this shared journey. For Cindi Mayweather, in many ways the quintessential Afrofuturist subject, time is her battleground, and time travel her arsenal's essential tool.

There is, throughout *The ArchAndroid*, the running theme of running out of time. The impatient pace of "Dance or Die" and "Faster" underscores the need to stay one step ahead of Droid Control. "Neon Valley Street" sees Cindi and Anthony "running fast through time" together, trying perhaps to find someplace far from their own world where "the time was wrong" and their love could not yet be accepted.

The third movement of "BaBopByeYa," the album's nearly nine-minute finale, makes clear the power of time, and the importance of controlling it. The music slows, making space for Cindi's measured spoken word as she addresses Anthony Greendown. Time has slowed too, allowing Cindi to live in her memories, memorizing her separated lover's every detail. Anthony has made a home in Cindi's memory, and "there [he] will abide for forever." Though "now somewhere time pursues" them, it is in these lovers' ability to control time, to "rewind the clock," that their love shines. For what is a powerful love if not timeless?

We measure the greatness of love by its ability to exist outside of time, and for Cindi that ability lies not only in the realm of memory and sentiment. As could be seen in the "Tightrope" music video, weaponized time travel is the domain of the Great Divide, who routinely plucks revolutionaries out of time to be kept in the Palace of the Dogs. These suppressive methods are revisited in the music video for a later single, "Q.U.E.E.N.," in which visitors are welcomed to the Living Museum, where the Time Council (a Ministry of Droids subset, all agents of the Great Divide) captures legendary rebels and puts them on display in suspended animation. One such exhibit houses the members of Wondaland and their notorious leader Janelle Monáe, apprehended for their twenty-first-century musical weapons program. Monáe and her accomplices are quickly freed, brought back to life through the playing of a "Q.U.E.E.N." record.

Much like the brief escape from the Palace of the Dogs in "Tightrope," the power to subvert the Great Divide's actions and harness time for herself is Monáe's for the taking. Cindi's, too, but here we see the blurring between artist and alter ego that has made Monáe such an intriguing proposition. If part of Cindi Mayweather's story is that she is partially cloned from Janelle Monáe, and that Monáe herself is a citizen of Metropolis cast aside and sent back in time to the twenty-first century, where does story end and reality begin?

"There's a time travelling machine here," said Monáe of Atlanta, when speaking to the *Guardian* in 2014. "OutKast have been through it, I've been through it, a lot of the artists have been through it. It was created for Atlanta. And there's an underwater world here called New Atlantis that also has an area where you can travel back and forth." It is but one of many allusions Monáe has made to not being of our time in her media appearances, and it is easy to see that refusal to separate Cindi from Janelle as beautifully Afrofuturistic. The art itself has no need for the distinctions of past and future; it is fed from the legacy of those artists and thinkers that came before while facing squarely forward toward the future. Why should the artist be any different? If filtering Monáe's message through the character of Cindi Mayweather strengthens it, why make clear where the fantasy begins and ends?

"We've always seen ourselves in relation to a continuum of freedom fighters and people who wanted to make sure that love had a place in the future, that peace had a place in the future," said Chuck Lightning in a Greg Tate-moderated panel at Moogfest 2016. "That's the thing that I really love about this rubric that people call Afrofuturism, I think it's just a tribe of really brave motherfuckers." At its heart, Afrofuturism is an act of care, care for community, for ancestry, for the opportunity to grow into a future waiting with open arms. *The ArchAndroid* is a template, a way forward that guides listeners along Monáe's own path to power, with all the doubt and missteps that make up this still-ongoing adventure. This is Monáe's Afrofuturist project, enacted through Cindi, because of Cindi, as Cindi. The two cannot be separated, forging a path for all of us as twin guides, artist and art, dreamer and dream.

3
Oh, Maker

We don't create a fantasy world to escape reality,
we create it to be able to stay.
—*Lynda Barry*[1]

In "Far Beyond the Stars," a season-six episode of *Star Trek: Deep Space Nine*, Captain Benjamin Sisko is contemplating stepping down from his position and letting someone else "make the tough calls" in the ongoing war with the imperialist Dominion. He feels, justifiably, that he is "carrying the weight of the entire Alpha Quadrant on [his] shoulders," and is eager for respite.

Soon into the episode, Sisko begins hallucinating images of 1950s New York, eventually finding himself in the life of Black science fiction writer Benny Russell. Unlike typical *Star Trek* episodes that feature time travel, however, here Sisko has no memory of his twenty-fourth-century existence.

[1] *What It Is.* Used with permission from the author and Drawn & Quarterly Books Inc.

He fully inhabits Russell's life as the writer attempts to make his mark at *Incredible Tales* magazine—a publication whose racist owners are equally committed to letting their readership believe in an all-white writing staff by concealing photographic evidence of the magazine's "negro with a typewriter."

The story alternates between Sisko, increasingly desperate to address these hallucinations, and Russell, busy fighting for his right to publish a story about a Black twenty-fourth-century captain and his beautiful free-floating space station, despite editors and publishers who deem the work unbelievable. Russell fields opposition from all sides, another Black man proclaiming, "the only reason they'll ever let us in space is if they need someone to shine their shoes." No one, it seems, believes in Russell's vision. No one will see what he sees.

Russell, bombarded with professional discrimination and police brutality, eventually concedes to a rewrite of the ending, making *Deep Space Nine* nothing but a dream and watering down the story in an effort to get it published. But even this proves to be fruitless, and the entire issue is pulped. Star Avery Brooks gives a gutting performance, crumbling as his dream is taken away. Metatextually, the tragedy is felt even more keenly: because the audience has watched Benjamin Sisko lead his crew for six seasons, knows that Russell's imagined future can, and does, in fact exist, the injustice stings all the more.

The boundaries between the two stories blur, made more porous by the regular *Trek* cast also taking on roles in Russell's story. Russell, too, begins seeing flashes of Sisko's life. These visions only spur him on, as does the advice of a street preacher: "Write those words, brother Benny, let them see the glory of what lies ahead."

Grieving the death of a friend and increasingly distressed, Russell's story comes to an end with a powerful, harrowing speech:

> You can deny me all you want, but you cannot deny Ben Sisko. He exists. That future, that space station, all those people, they exist in here, in my mind. I created it. . . . You can pulp a story, but you cannot destroy an idea. Don't you understand? That's ancient knowledge. You cannot destroy an idea. That future, I created it, and it's real!

Russell continues to repeat "I created it" and "It's real" as he is carried out on a stretcher, tears streaming down his face as he clings to the certainty that this miraculous world flung far into the future is possible despite the unrelenting tragedy of his own life. Now wearing Sisko's uniform, Russell's last sight is of the street preacher, improbably joining him in the ambulance for one final message: "You are the dreamer and the dream."

Sisko wakes, in a poignant reversal of the dream ending in Russell's story, with renewed clarity and purpose. He will not be giving up his command. But all is not so easily resolved. In a conversation with his father, played by the same actor as the street preacher, Sisko wonders whether his time as Benny Russell was a dream at all. He asks, "What if this life we're leading, all of this, you and me, everything, what if all of this is the illusion? . . . Maybe Benny isn't the dream. We are." This line of questioning casts the entirety of the show in a much different light, turning what has up until this point been a simple nineties science fiction spinoff into what is potentially the hope-giving, lifesaving, fantasy of someone in the audience's past. Though the distinction of who is "real" is ultimately unimportant as *Deep Space Nine* continues on unimpeded, the episode presents a fascinating exploration of the boundary between dream and dreamer, a border constantly in flux. All Sisko can do is live his life while acknowledging that "for all we know, at this very moment, somewhere far beyond all those distant stars, Benny Russell is dreaming of us."

"Far Beyond the Stars" represents a departure from usual *Star Trek* conventions. Unlike the franchise's usually "deracinated use of history," here the stakes are all too personal and all too real, removing what De Witt Douglas Kilgore terms the "cognitive distance Starfleet officers often face."[2] That Benny Russell doesn't remember even being Benjamin Sisko, that he exists in a fully realized world of colleagues, friends, and lovers, sets him apart from other alter egos adopted by *Trek* characters when the spatial anomaly of the day has hurled them back in time.

Benny Russell stands as an anchor, a reminder of the journey that had to be undertaken to get to Sisko's relative utopia.[3] It's a trajectory that is invaluable to Avery Brooks, who in 1994 discussed playing Sisko with *TV Guide*:

[2] "'The Best Is Yet to Come'; or, Saving the Future: *Star Trek Deep Space Nine* as Reform Astrofuturism."

[3] Sisko's sense of belonging within history is also evident in season seven's "Badda-Bing, Badda-Bang." In that episode, he (initially) refuses to join a

For me, this is as hard-core as it gets: Because I am brown and American and male, it is important for me—and for our brown children everywhere—to be able to think in the long term. Today many of our children, especially males, do not project that they will live past the age of 19 or 20. *Star Trek* allows our children the chance to see something they might not otherwise imagine. My life's work has always been about making a way for succeeding generations.

Brooks, in playing the first Black captain in a *Star Trek* series, is exceedingly aware of the power that can be found in imagining oneself into the future. Standing as he is between Russell and Sisko, Brooks's project is an Afrofuturist one, simultaneously aware of the past but looking to the future. "Far Beyond the Stars" in particular makes literal the power of such a dream, with Russell functionally creating the reality that Sisko inhabits.

A similar push and pull exists between Janelle Monáe and Cindi Mayweather, with Monáe occupying the middle ground between honored past and imagined future. In a *Fast Company* interview in 2018, she outlined her involvement in a Michelle Obama-headed voter registration campaign, stating that her "grandparents didn't have the right to vote.

---

popular holosuite program set in an ahistorically tolerant pre–Civil Rights Movement Las Vegas, uncomfortable in the knowledge that he would never have been allowed entry into the establishments of the real thing. "We cannot ignore the truth about our past," says Sisko, who despite the intervening centuries is still respectful of the struggle for civil rights and none too keen to erase it.

[Her] mother came up at the end of segregation." Her work, she continued, was a way of paying tribute to her family, including a recently departed grandmother. Michelle Obama herself is quoted in the article as saying that Monáe "never forgets where she came from," something likewise expressed in a bio on Monáe's website ahead of *Electric Lady*'s release: "I also wanted to figure out how to take Kansas City to the future . . . like a surreal Parliament album with lyrics by Octavia Butler and album art by Salvador Dalí." For Monáe, all methods of reaching one's desired destination, whether political or musical, involve a firm knowledge of where one has been.

"Oh, Maker" stands out as *The ArchAndroid*'s best attempt at putting Monáe and Cindi in conversation. Though the liner notes cite Katharine Burnheart—architect of the Alpha Platinum 9000 line—as the maker in question, one can easily place Monáe, Cindi's animating force in more ways than one, as intended interlocutor. As both the artist responsible for Cindi's creation and, textually, Cindi's genetic source code, Monáe is directly responsible for the making of Cindi. In this melancholy song, dream addresses dreamer, wanting so badly to find meaning in her existence.

With a bittersweet guitar bringing *Sounds of Silence* to mind, "Oh, Maker" begins with "I hear the drizzle of the rain"—the same line that opens the Simon & Garfunkel classic "Kathy's Song." A similar longing can be found in both songs, but where Paul Simon is focused on romantic love, Cindi yearns for an altogether more existential rapprochement.

Simon's penultimate verse tells of bewilderment ("And so you see I have come to doubt / All that I once held as true /

I stand alone without beliefs"), assuaged by love ("The only truth I know is you"). In the context of a doubting cyborg, that search for faith and certainty takes on a different, more devout, sheen. The other references for "Oh, Maker" cited in the liner notes include Frankenstein's Monster and Rabbi Loew's Golem, archetypal monstrous entities created by man but denied self-determination and an equitable place within their communities. It follows that Cindi would be eager to establish a relationship with her creator, be they divine or of this earth, in her attempt to balance her programming with her greater purpose.

In "Kathy's Song," the speaker watches raindrops "weave their weary paths and die" on the windowpane, knowing that if it was not for the love of the titular Kathy, "there but for the grace of you go I." Cindi, too, is "really lost, baby," disoriented by the amount of hurt she has witnessed in the world. She finds strength in the fact that her maker must have loved her to create her, and that she in turn can reciprocate that love. As she finishes her song and continues her journey, she knows that she does so with her maker's love in her pocket, and eyes in her soul.

*   *   *

In a 2010 episode of the *All Things Considered* podcast, Monáe relays that much of *The ArchAndroid*'s music came to her in dream form. "This was the first time when I was working on a project that songs came to me in my dreams," she says. "As soon as I would get up it was like, 'Oh man this song was absolutely gorgeous. I cannot panic or I'm going to forget the string arrangements, I'm going to forget how my voice is supposed to sound." In much the same way as Monáe's relationship to Cindi blurs the boundaries between creator and creation, Monáe's dreams are proof of a much more fluid relationship between maker and vessel. "You have to listen to what your maker is saying," she says. "That I think is very important as an artist." But the question of who the maker is doesn't always have a clear answer. Monáe might describe her storytelling abilities as something provided from on high, but in the same interview also says, "I think the characters in Metropolis were moving through me, and I had to expose them." Is it Cindi's ability to time travel that allows her to communicate through dreams, making sure her story is told at the time when it is most needed? And if the residents of Metropolis, chief among them Cindi, are the ones controlling the show, who then is the dreamer, and who the dream?

In *Pitchfork*'s review of *The ArchAndroid*, Matthew Perpetua writes that Monáe's "imagination and iconography deepen the record as an experience and give her license to go far out, but it ultimately serves as a fun, flashy framework for pop songs with universal lyrical sentiments." Though Perpetua has almost got it right, he misses how the fantasy element of *The ArchAndroid*—the specificity of its Metropolis setting and all the characters who inhabit it—offers crucial context to the sentiments expressed in the songs. Yes, there is universality to the music, a conscious decision made by a creative team unwilling to get bogged down in detail in its search for highly danceable songs. But remove Metropolis and something essential is lost. Cindi's loves and struggles are not merely a framing device but a foundational part of the album. The yearning bone-deep love of "BaBopByeYa," though beautiful in its own right, can fully be felt only if one has followed Cindi and Anthony across the preceding songs. Any less than the full context diminishes the emotional resonance. Without Metropolis finding its way into Monáe's dreams, there is no *ArchAndroid*.

It is certainly possible to enjoy the album solely on the merits of its earworm melodies and plethora of hooks, and many do. Large-scale themes and larger-than-life orchestral arrangements will sweep up a casual listener on a more than satisfactory ride, but for faithful ArchAndroid converts there is plenty of paratextual information to be found. Cindi's backstory in particular benefits from some fleshing out with the help of *The ArchAndroid*'s liner notes and Monáe's still extant 57821.tumblr.com. For example Katharine Burnheart, author of the "Alpha Platinum 9000 journals," receives a mention in the liner notes for "Oh, Maker," but then disappears from the story completely for years. It is only closer to *Electric Lady*'s release that the Tumblr reveals more.

Functioning as a diegetic analysis of Samuel Spratt's *Electric Lady* album cover, 57821.tumblr.com provides background information about the world of Metropolis in the guise of an in-world analysis of the art. The album cover, a painting hanging in the "Royal Black House in the aspect of Metropolis known as New Atlantis," is titled "Cindi Mayweather and Her Sisters Cast a Spell Over the Good City of Metropolis." The 2717 painting—noteworthy, according to Time University scholars, in its depiction of Cindi before

Figure 4   The album cover for *Electric Lady* (© 2013 Sam Spratt/
Bad Boy Records, LLC).

she became a "cybersoul superstar"—shows Cindi with her
five identical sisters[4] posing, startled, around a glowing metal
skull.]

---

[4] Named Andromeda, Andy Pisces, Catalina, Morovia, and Polly Whynot
(in a cool little homage to William Klein's 1966 New Wave film *Qui êtes-vous, Polly Magoo?*, the main visual inspiration for the album cover).

This is the legendary Skull of Night Thrashings, the first fully functional Alpha Platinum 9000 cranium built by inventor Katharine Burnheart. Now in the possession of Wolfmaster Number 1, President, King, and Lord Oddpa Crix, the skull gives Cindi's backstory more heft. Though she will be elevated above others by her music career, Cindi is very much one of a much larger set, and much longer lineage. The skull, a common motif in the *vanitas* still lifes of sixteenth- and seventeenth-century paintings, emphasizes Cindi's cyborg nature by evoking both the fleeting mortality of organic life, and her constructed, machinic android parts.

For those curious listeners eager for more of Cindi's story than the songs themselves provide, the minutiae of the Metropolis mythos is there for the discovering. As *ArchAndroid* concept artist Chad Weatherford puts it, there's a "full on backstory, and you're just given crumbs." We might be left guessing, when reading the liner notes for "Cold War," what "Martin McKnight's famous 'I Have a Scream' speech" might mean (beyond the winking MLK reference), but more of the Metropolis saga quickly falls into place when reading the Tumblr. There we learn that Martin McKnight is, like Katharine Burnheart, also an inventor, one known primarily for creating the Drogon. A fabled robotic dragon built during World War C, legends say that the Drogon lies dormant, awaiting the advent of the ArchAndroid to finally wake and bring "a fiery end to the reign of the Wolfmasters and the Great Divide." We may never know if there is truth to these legends, but on the cover of *The ArchAndroid* Cindi can be seen wearing Drogon's symbol, his blue glowing eyes a rallying point for droids fighting for justice, liberation, and pride.

According to Weatherford, Drogon's symbol was simply part of the initial sketch. "There was never really a thought at the time about what it was," he told me, but given that it was such a prominent part of the concept for Cindi's crown, "Chuck in particular fixated on it. We'd have discussions, 'Oh that could be the skull of the first android' or something of that nature, and then it evolved into the dragon." Given the vastness and eclecticism of the Metropolis mythology, it comes as no surprise that the world's lore evolved organically, a sort of ad hoc free association based on the music, art, and literature surrounding Monáe and her collaborators. There is no knowing how Cindi's story will continue to be filled in, no way to anticipate how Metropolis will continue to grow and transform and come to life.

* * *

"Places are never just places in a piece of writing," says Carmen Maria Machado in her memoir *In the Dream House*. "If they are, the author has failed. Setting is not inert. It is activated by point of view." One of *The ArchAndroid*'s greatest strengths is undoubtedly the world building of Metropolis itself and the ways in which music and lyrics create the perfect fantastical backdrop for an android's high-drama struggle for freedom. Brought to life by the story playing out within its confines, Metropolis functions as its own character in Cindi's journey, amorphous and difficult to pin down, but key to understanding the story and its stakes.

Metropolis is a sprawl of ambiguity. The city at once houses elves, aliens, androids, and humans: a coexistence that, from what we see of Cindi's story, is tenuous at best. While epic in scope, Metropolis is unlike other grand fantasy narratives in that it is purposefully haphazard in its distribution of the details (this writer, at least, would love to comb through *Lord of the Rings*-style maps and appendices, though the official paratext of liner notes, YouTube uploads, and Tumblr posts is admittedly quite enough to be getting along with). The megacity is at once the surreal garden of delights of "Wondaland" and the mean streets of "Dance or Die." In other albums, it's the smoky, sensual Electric Sheep Nightclub seen in the "PrimeTime" music video, and the shiny, sinister android auction of "Many Moons."

J. R. R. Tolkien, in his work of criticism *On Fairy Stories*, offers a useful lens through which to view Metropolis and its incongruous assemblage of places, aesthetics, and meanings. Tolkien's archetypal world beyond our own, Faërie, "cannot be caught in a net of words." Faërie is indescribable, if not imperceptible; a fantasyland one feels rather than dissects. Analysis "will not necessarily discover the secret of the whole." It is a place of peril, a place where fantasies are not guaranteed to be beautiful or safe, but a place with emancipatory potential. Metropolis is a feeling, unconstrained by geography and existing out of time.

The Neon Valley Street district, however, serves as anchor location. Mentioned in the earliest moments of *Metropolis: The Chase Suite* as the place a certain love-struck cyborg "now scheduled for immediate disassembly"[5] can be found,

---

[5] "The March of the Wolfmasters."

the district is a home under threat, with a horde of bounty hunters armed with chainsaws and electrodaggers fast approaching.

But the Neon Valley Street we return to in *The ArchAndroid* is not the same site of crisis. Smoothly transitioning out of Suite III's overture with the dreamiest of strings ("That John Williams string arrangement" another gift from Monáe's dreams),[6] the central feeling is one of yearning. It is now clear that Cindi and Anthony are currently separated, Cindi using her music to reach out to her beloved, repeating over and over her wish for a song capable of reaching Anthony's heart. It is a longing that infiltrates every aspect of the song, down to its credits in the liner notes: Monáe's lyrics are "lovesick," her lead vocals "pining," and Wonder's bass guitar "hearthumping."

Featuring wistful interpolations of Rodgers and Hart's "With a Song in My Heart" from the 1930 musical film *Spring Is Here*, "Neon Valley Street" is a song couched in nostalgia. The romance of "With a Song in My Heart" is immediate, the singer reveling in it: "When the music swells / I'm touching your hand / it tells that you're standing here." Cindi's version, in comparison, exists only in the past. Our android will have to content herself with memories, singing "for now I'll pretend / I'm holding your hand."

Neon Valley Street is a place of both danger and of possibility, which of course makes it a convenient synecdoche for Metropolis itself. With luxurious orchestration and

---

[6] *All Things Considered*, 2010.

gentle, earnest vocals, Cindi's song is able to "journey on," a phenomenon unto itself. A medium acting as its own message. When Cindi sings "may the sound of my voice be your guide" she is acting as both Anthony's lover and as the ArchAndroid, offering all of the district's residents a way forward in love, if they will only allow themselves to "love the sweet melody" and "bathe in the noise."

The song's breakdown is an intimate address. This is Cindi speaking directly to Anthony, the lover with whom she runs "fast through time like [Harriet] Tubman and John Henry." That Monáe has cast Cindi and Anthony in these historic roles is significant. Henry and Tubman both function as symbols of perseverance in extreme circumstances in the public imagination. John Henry, a hero immortalized in folk ballads and work songs, was a steel driver who sought to prove his superiority by racing a steam-powered drill brought in to replace him. The story ends with Henry winning against the machine, only to die of heart failure with his hammer still in his hand. Tubman, for her part, should need no introduction. The emancipatory abolitionist, activist, spy, and Underground Railroad conductor was responsible for freeing over seventy enslaved people, her life now the subject of much attention (including a 2019 biopic featuring Monáe herself in a supporting role). Tubman and Henry's accomplishments are of interest here not only because they are remarkable but because of how mythologized the two historical figures have become. Both have taken on a larger-than-life character that transcends their own time, effectively becoming time travelers through their ongoing legacy.

The conflict facing these separated lovers is timeless as well. Cindi's mention of "atomic blues bombing hearts" speaks to the emotional repercussions of living under Metropolis's siege, while allusions to both the 2003 Iraq invasion and Babylon—the megacity of antiquity—make clear that the violence of the Great Divide has always existed. Conflicts, whether ancient or contemporary, always stem from the same hate.

Piano chords pulse like stars underneath Kellindo Parker's electric guitar, which takes over for Cindi in the last minute and a half of the song. Liner notes for "Neon Valley Street" confirm that the song is inspired by "Cindi's last thoughts before entering cybertronic purgatory (July 18, 2719)." Suspended on softly fading guitar, these are the last moments before entering a new life. On her way to reincarnation as the ArchAndroid Cindi's thoughts, of course, are of love.

"Fairy-stories deal largely," writes Tolkien, "with simple or fundamental things." Any fantasy world worthy of attention has at its core a universal truth, or an essential feeling. A metaphor without a central message will spiral outward, uncontrolled and ineffective. If Cindi's story has one unified message, it is the reminder to love in the face of hate. It is a simple sentiment, but one that holds great power and is too often forgotten. Neon Valley Street and, more broadly, Metropolis function as an archetypal hostile world where the lesson is that much more important to learn. As Tolkien writes, "these simplicities are made all the more luminous by their setting." If love can and must be found in a place as loveless as Metropolis, then there can be no excuse not to pursue love in our own worlds and own lives.

*   *   *

Suite III offers an interesting, if perhaps non-linear, progression in Cindi's journey. After "Neon Valley Street" come "Make the Bus" and "Wondaland," songs that continue to explore Cindi's relationships to herself and her world. Together they act as a blueprint of sorts, Cindi learning how to integrate being the ArchAndroid into her life.

Though there is perhaps a more direct narrative at play, I have always preferred to think of each album in the Cindi Mayweather saga as more of a snapshot of a particular moment in the story. The albums create pictures—more driven by emotion than by plot—that produce a cohesive vision that is perhaps better at imparting the truth when not squeezed into more accessible story beats. In the spirit of other notable concept albums like *Sgt. Pepper's Lonely Hearts Club Band* or *Tommy*, the concept provides a loose framework, one often requiring paratextual explanation.

In *Metropolis: The Chase Suite*, Cindi is introduced in medias res at a time of great crisis. The broad strokes of her background, her romance, and her criminality are provided. In *The ArchAndroid*, those moments are expanded, and we see an android on the run and grappling with the implications of her decisions and her destiny. *Electric Lady* finds Cindi now much more sure of her power, with the framing device of the radio segments showing how the general Metropolis population is dealing with the advent of a messiah. In many ways *Electric Lady* is to external conflict what *The ArchAndroid* is to the exploration of Cindi's internal landscape.

Tolkien writes that fantasy "certainly does not destroy or even insult Reason," neither blunting one's appetite for reason nor obscuring one's perception of it. "On the contrary," he writes. "The keener and clearer is the reason, the better fantasy will it make." Even when the Metropolis saga seems to move through time nonsensically, prompting more questions than are ever answered—What is cybertronic purgatory? Did Cindi go there at the end of the "Many Moons" video? Did she go back at the end of "Neon Valley Street"? Do both songs describe the same visit? How does she get out? *Does* she get out?—there is still reason. There is still a deeper truth being explored. *The ArchAndroid* may have little interest in answering every question, but the album's core dialogue—on the importance of harnessing one's own power, or balancing pleasure and responsibility, or fighting injustice no matter the cost—remains secure. Besides, progress itself is never linear, and it stands to reason an album charting one android's path to technomessianic ascension would feature some twists and turns.

Thus we come to *The ArchAndroid*'s least in-house offering, "Make the Bus." Written, composed, arranged, produced, and partially sung by Of Montreal front man Kevin Barnes, "Make the Bus" can be seen as a discussion Cindi is having with herself, a conversation between conflicting impulses. The song's opening lines of "the way you are now / You're never gonna make the bus" suggest Erykah Badu's "Bag Lady," in which Monáe's future collaborator sings "bag lady you gon' miss your bus / You can't hurry up, 'cause you got too much stuff." Badu, listed in the liner notes as one of the song's inspirations, entreats her listener not to take past baggage into new relationships, believing that "one day all them bags gon' get in your way," so it's best to "pack light." The eponymous bag lady is incapable of shedding her baggage, having never been told that "all you must hold onto, is you."

The way Cindi is now, she's never going to succeed, never going to make the bus. Our nascent ArchAndroid is still struggling with Badu's baggage, still unwilling to fully commit to the sacrifices becoming the ArchAndroid will require. Much must still be done before Cindi is ready to save anyone, even herself. Barnes's singing here acts as a sort of check and balance, as he refuses to follow the "everyone" who is so impressed with how Cindi is dealing with the existential questions facing android-kind. Cindi may have "*Do Androids Dream of Electric Sheep?* under [her] pillow," truly the perfect bedtime reading for a budding robot revolutionary, but Barnes-as-narrator remains unmoved. It won't be enough to read the texts and pay lip service to the ideas, Cindi will have to walk the walk, and remake herself entirely if she is to succeed.

With Barnes and Monáe singing in unison for much of the song, it is easy to interpret this duet as internal conflict, the use of "we" and "our" further aligning both vocalists. Barnes seems to function as Cindi's chastising super-ego, ready to whip a distracted, love-addled id into shape. Without an ego to balance between the two, the relationship is dominant, Barnes pointing out her more thoughtlessly childish whims— say, spitting on people from above as Peter Pan—but also engaging in such behavior himself by "standing over [her] eating juicy fruits till it gets in [her] eye." The chorus often, both at the beginning of the song and after the bridge, elides the beat between lines. It is an overlap that, along with the clock strikes opening the song, creates a cramped feeling—the feeling of thoughts swirling and chasing one another.

In this confused state, Cindi's "terrible fixation," the thing she can't get off her mind, might very well be becoming the ArchAndroid. It's something she's as of yet unwilling to "get to know better," preferring to "keep in in the realm of fantasy" where actual commitment is unnecessary. And if Barnes's vocals signify the part of Cindi destined for divinity, the part fighting to leave behind worldly attachments, it's a part that is losing patience. "You wanted me just for a holiday / Or was it to pad your resume," rebukes Barnes, growing tired of Cindi's vacillations.

A small chaos of looped cymbals and bar chimes leads us into "Wondaland," a world of fantasy where all are welcome provided they keep its secrets. The song captures much of the underlying ethos of *The ArchAndroid*, namely, that the desiring and the divine can find balance and exist together. Wondaland is a place of pleasure that Cindi desperately wishes to go back to, to be taken back to. Wondaland is where desire, passion, connection, creativity, and art thrive. Lyrics like "let me paint your canvas as you dance" reference Monáe's tendency in her earlier shows to paint the same silhouette of a woman partway through her set (to the point where she now apparently has hundreds of these portraits in storage). Almost a compulsion, Monáe brought up the practice in therapy, eventually naming the figure the Electric

Lady: a boundary-breaking female archetype for the twenty-first century. The paintings usually came into being during performances of "Mushrooms & Roses," the song during which Cindi is most explicitly in Wondaland. "Wondaland" the song, for its part, acts as more an analysis of that haven, articulating the desire to return to it.

Wondaland is a carnal place, and when backup vocals assure us that a "magnificent droid plays there," it's unclear whether it is music or love games being played. Extended synth chords float over a chorus that ends with "she thinks she left her underpants," sometimes sung as "you know she left her underpants." Cindi would very much like to spend the night, and in Wondaland there are no walks of shame in the morning.

There is divinity in Cindi's desire, and no sin nor disgrace mars the perfect shelter of Wondaland. To drive this point home, the song's bridge and outro sample hallelujahs from "All Creatures of Our God and King," by cleric and hymn-writer Thomas Ken. Ken's hymn finds the divine in the natural world, from the "silver moon with softer gleam" to the "rushing wind that art so strong." It is a rapturous celebration of the physical world and its ability to bring the heavenly closer, a perfect underscoring of what makes "Wondaland" so special. The hallelujahs, paired with animal sounds and layered ethereal voices credited as being "faerie" vocals, all add to this heady mix of the primal and the transcendent. In the midst of her passion, Cindi embodies both these aspects, singing, "I think I'm a love angel" (sometimes heard as "I think I'm in love, angel" to blur whether Cindi herself is, or is merely communing with, the divine).

This is the world Cindi struggles to survive and uplift. Metropolis is the physical and the holy, the danger and the safe haven, dystopia and utopia, Neon Valley Street and Wondaland. The work that is needed to bring balance to this deeply divided world is as complex and multifaceted as the work needed to better our own. In showing how Cindi plans to lead a city so difficult to pin down, Monáe offers us what is perhaps the only blueprint capable of encompassing all that we need do to make our own world more just.

When accepting a National Book Foundation award in 1973, science fiction author Ursula K. Le Guin proposed realism as "perhaps the least adequate means of understanding or portraying the incredible realities of our existence." To understand, fully understand, our world one must acknowledge that, "as great scientists have said and as all children know, it is above all by the imagination that we achieve perception, and compassion, and hope." Accepting another such award in 2014, Le Guin continued:

> I think hard times are coming when we will be wanting the voices of writers who can see alternatives to how we live now and can see through our fear-stricken society and its obsessive technologies to other ways of being, and even imagine some real grounds for hope. We will need writers who can remember freedom: Poets, visionaries, the realists of a larger reality.

The work of fantasy and science fiction, of speculative fiction in all its forms, is to question, to probe, to wonder about the ifs and the whys of things. It is something Le Guin believed in strongly, and Monáe seems to have a genius for. Metropolis is a case study. It is a far-future, magical experiment with real real-world implications.

In her essay "World-Making," Le Guin's "idea of making makes [her] think of making new. Making a new world, a different world"—like Tolkien's Middle Earth or her own deep space societies—but it also makes her think of "making the world new: making the world different." Science fiction is the work of the political imagination, a theoretical practice that can warn against (the dystopia) or teach better (the utopia). Monáe is doing both. Within the framework of Metropolis lie the answers to our every question. Though those answers may not be straightforward, everything we must avoid and everything we must work toward can be found within this made-up world, this fantasy created by someone who wishes to create a better future. Monáe is Benny Russell writing Benjamin Sisko, and Sisko dreaming Russell. She is the world builder bringing Metropolis to life in our reality, and allowing us in turn the opportunity to see our reality within Metropolis. "An artist makes the world her world," writes Le Guin. "An artist makes her world the world. For a little while. For a long as it takes to look at or listen to or watch or read the work of art." For eighteen songs at least, Metropolis is open to us, and there is so much to be found inside.

4
Come Alive

As a culture worker who belongs to an oppressed people
my job is to make revolution irresistible.
—*Toni Cade Bambara*[1]

"Early each morning he searched for her, 'til his feet became bloody and tired'" begins "57821." With vocals provided by Monáe, Wonder, and Lightning (the latter two known as Deep Cotton when singing as a duo), this is Anthony Greendown's song. The beloved is searching for his lover, clutching hologram photo and lock of hair close as he finds his way to a chained 57821, "cold in the cell, lost and shivering."

A 1960s-inspired folk rock ballad,[2] "57821" tells of Anthony's journey to find a captured Cindi, imprisoned in

---

[1] From an interview conducted by Kay Bonetti for the American Audio Prose Library, Inc., in *Conversations with Toni Cade Bambara*, edited by Thabiti Lewis. University Press of Mississippi, 2012. Copyright © 1982. Used with permission from the American Audio Prose Library, Inc.

[2] Love's Arthur Lee is listed as one of the song's liner note inspirations.

the dark with only the sounds of gunshots for company. In only two verses, Anthony is able to find Cindi, rescue her, and encourage her to persevere as he sings that she must continue to fight "like Achilles in Troy." Cindi is Anthony's sun, brilliant even in the darkness, but as much as Anthony is focused on his love for Cindi, he also realizes her power as the ArchAndroid. Her light is not for him alone. "I saved you so you'd save the world," he tells her, offering as a sort of prayer: "May your light lead them both back to one."

Harkening back to Fritz Lang's *Metropolis* and the joining of the haves and the have-nots, Anthony seems committed to acting as aide, a Maria to Cindi's Freder. Anthony's role will be to help the hero onward to victory and transformation, and the Maria parallel can also be seen in his attempt to mythologize Cindi's story. As he sings one of the most lyrically direct songs of the album, he is both the android's inspiration and her apostle, spreading the word of Cindi. And if that word is a familiar one, the liner notes make clear why: One of the listed inspirations for "57821" is *The Hero with a Thousand Faces*, Joseph Campbell's treatise on the monomyth.

The monomyth, or Hero's Journey, functions as a common story template, a recognizable pattern characterized by a sequence of steps regularly undertaken by a hero in many of the world's mythologies. These steps will often include a call to action, a series of challenges, a transformation, and a return to the hero's "known" world. In this way, "57821" charts an archetypal journey, the song telling at least a portion of a timeless story.

In the original *Star Wars* trilogy, one of the more recognizable contemporary examples of the monomyth, a hero named Skywalker is called to action by a mysterious princess's distress signal. This call leads him into a previously unknown world where he learns to become the hero—or Jedi knight—he was always destined to be. It's of little surprise that "57821" also lists "the blue of Luke's lightsaber" as one of its inspirations.

It is that iconic blue that provides insight into where the song falls in Cindi's story. The young boy from Tatooine uses that color lightsaber only in the earlier parts of his story. Once Luke has become a fully fledged Jedi, he crafts himself a new weapon that gives off a green light. The blue lightsaber, once belonging to father and sworn enemy Darth Vader, signals an unfinished journey, and potential still untapped. Anthony, in the song's lyrics, says as much when he sings "here's the book, now the saga's begun." Even this late in *The ArchAndroid*, Cindi's story is only at its beginning.

In *The Hero with a Thousand Faces*, Campbell describes his archetypal protagonist as someone who "ventures forth from the world of common day into a region of supernatural wonder." Once there, "fabulous forces" are encountered and a victory is won. Finally, "the hero comes back from this mysterious adventure with the power to bestow boons on his fellow man." It is a simple story, self-contained and with a clear linear progression that has served many stories, *Star Wars* included, well. "57821" in many ways offers the same satisfying sense of completion, even if the song covers only a short portion of Cindi's story. It's easy to imagine that what comes after the setback of imprisonment will be nothing but triumph, paving the way to a glorious climax, a showdown with the evil forces that sought to suppress our dear Cindi. But from what we know of Cindi, of the ArchAndroid, of Metropolis and all the contradictions it encompasses, a simple story seems hardly sufficient. "57821" may be inspired by the Hero's Journey, but as we have seen from the songs that come directly from Cindi, this straightforward template cannot hope to contain the complexities of the story Monáe is telling.

Instead, the story of the ArchAndroid is one that has many real-world equivalents. It is a malleable metaphor, with explorations of Metropolis capable of shedding light on much of what is wrong with our world. And the world Cindi inhabits, too, is richer, stronger, when viewed as a response to the real world of her creator, when the android's struggles are contextualized by the world in which Monáe exists.

In her work *Pleasure Activism*, adrienne maree brown writes that all political organizing, all work done to counter injustice, is science fictional at its core. "We are shaping a future we long for and have not yet experienced," she writes. "We are in an imagination battle, and almost everything about how we orient toward our bodies is shaped by fearful imaginations. Imaginations that fear Blackness, brownness, fatness, queerness, disability, difference." This radical imagination is, according to brown, a necessary weapon for "reclaiming our right to shape our lived reality."

Cindi's tumultuous journey from cloned worker and synthetic commodity to cybersoul superstar, then criminalized lover, hunted prey, and technomessiah, cannot hope to bend itself into the shape of the Hero's Journey. Despite the simplified narrative Anthony creates in his attempts at proselytization, the story is simply trying to say too much. But if we endeavor to see the ways in which *The ArchAndroid*, in all its intricacies, is commenting on our own world, functioning as brown's radical imagination, we can begin to understand what story is really being told.

*   *   *

"This is kind of embarrassing for me," says Monáe as she attempts to set up an Instagram Live event in September 2020. There has already been a ten-minute delay due to technical difficulties for this, the first installment of her *Liberation & Elevation* series, a set of conversations with prominent Black women thinkers and activists presented in conjunction with the release of her film *Antebellum*. The normally poised pop multi-hyphenate is visibly annoyed with her inability to make the interview happen, a logical reaction for someone who has spent so much of her time in the public eye as a machine herself. "I talk about the future a lot, but technology sometimes . . ." she sighs, trailing off before lighting up as she finally connects with her inaugural interviewee, Black Lives Matter cofounder Patrisse Khan-Cullors.

Founded in 2013 after the acquittal of Trayvon Martin's murderer, Black Lives Matter is a US-, Canada-, and UK-based organization committed to affirming the humanity of Black people, and ending anti-Black racism and state and police brutality. In *When They Call You a Terrorist*, Khan-Cullors's memoir written with asha bandele, Khan-Cullors begins with a childhood marked by the abuses of power in law enforcement and the criminal justice system, laying the groundwork for what would later become global activism. "The goal is freedom," she writes of BLM's mission. "The goal is to live beyond fear. The goal is to end the occupation of our bodies and souls by the agents of a larger American culture that demonstrates daily how we don't matter."

It is a mission that explicitly seeks to take up the mantle of the Civil Rights Movement. When writing about the ongoing legacy of figures like Ida B. Wells and the Black Panther Party, Khan-Cullors states, "we were and are their progeny, called to pick up a torch no generation wants to or can ignore." That sense of lineage, of shouldering a mantle passed down through centuries, permeates much of Khan-Cullors's memoir, imbuing the struggles of the present with the strength and resilience of the past:

I am the thirteenth-generation progeny of people who survived the hulls of slave ships, survived the chains, the whips, the months laying in their own shit and piss. The human beings legislated as not human beings who watched their names, their languages, their Goddesses and Gods, the arc of their dances and beats of their songs, the majesty of their dreams, their very families snatched up and stolen, disassembled and discarded, and despite this built language and honored God and created movement and upheld love. What could they be but stardust, these people who refused to die, who refused to accept the idea that their lives did not matter, that their children's lives did not matter?

Black Lives Matter is thus a contemporary iteration of an ancient fight, a fight for what is right, what is deserved, and what is owed.

In her conversation with Monáe, Khan-Cullors describes their shared movement as "the embodiment of living out our freedom even when we're not free yet," speaking to the power of imagination that makes so much science fiction thinking, Monáe's included, essential. It's a sentiment Khan-Cullors has brought forward from her memoir as well. "We say we deserve another knowing, the knowing that comes when you assume your life will be long, will be vibrant, will be healthy," she writes. "We deserve to imagine a world without prisons or punishment, a world where they are not needed, a world rooted in mutuality. We deserve to at least aim for that."

The imaginative force behind Black Lives Matter, as described by Khan-Cullors at least, is rooted in the desire to create a world that does not yet exist, a world that many believe could not possibly exist. To fight for such a world is to have hope, to know that a just world will exist one day. Of course hope alone cannot bring about needed political change, but the present will never change without a vision of the future. It is the same hope that animates the very best of science fiction. Monáe, who has included the sci-fi symbolism of androids and time travel in so much of her music, makes that connection impossible to ignore when discussing her work with Khan-Cullors: "Black Lives Matter gives me the strength."

Two years after the founding of BLM, in 2015, Monáe released the protest song "Hell You Talmbout." The song was written and performed by the extended Wondaland community of Monáe, Lightning, Wonder, Roman GianArthur, George 2.0, Jidenna, and Alex Belle and Isis Valentino of St. Beauty. Forceful and unflagging, the song invokes the names of those who have died from racial violence, often at the hands of the police, a horrendous catalogue of loss set to heavy, relentless drums. Though the original featured the names of Sandra Bland, Eric Garner, Amadou Diallo, and Trayvon Martin, among others, an instrumental version was released as well, encouraging listeners to make their own—a grim but necessary exercise in filling in the blanks.

Upon the song's release, a statement was provided on Instagram, describing the song as a vessel carrying "the unbearable anguish of millions." Recorded to "channel the pain, fear, and trauma caused by the ongoing slaughter of our brothers and sisters," "Hell You Talmbout" explicitly challenges the apathy and negligence with which this ongoing tragedy is so often met. "Silence is our enemy," says the statement. "Sound is our weapon."

In the years between the releases of *Electric Lady* and *Dirty Computer*, there was still very little of the non-android Monáe out in the world. Though she had released her single "Yoga," been named a spokesperson for CoverGirl, and been featured on the hugely successful "We Are Young" by Fun, in 2015 she was still largely known for what Katie Presley of *All Things Considered* termed her "cosmic Space Age aesthetic." The departure of "Hell You Talmbout" from what the public previously knew of Monáe was substantial, prompting Presley, in her review of the song, to note how "there's nothing droidlike in how Monáe and her cohort perform the song. Voices crack and mics pop." Of interest to Presley is the lack of creative distance between performers and audience, a removal of the pop-android persona in favor of something rawer, less carefully considered: "What remains is an unadorned, visceral, undeniably earthbound piece of protest music."

Though "Hell You Talmbout" is a direct response to the realities of being Black in America, it is not the first time that Monáe has reacted musically to an environment of profound loss and danger. From the first moments of *The ArchAndroid*, as singer-songwriter-poet Saul Williams sets the scene of "Dance or Die" with his spoken word, Monáe introduces a world where people can "never dream, never win." Metropolis is a quagmire of stunted opportunity where "kids are killing kids and then the kids join the army," a lost land where "Hell You Talmbout" would not be out of place.

"Dance or Die" repurposes lyrics from Notorious B.I.G.'s "Gimme the Loot," contextualizing the violence faced by androids in Metropolis by drawing parallels to the New York City of 1994. In "Gimme the Loot," Biggie plays the part of a "robbery expert" planning future heists. Monáe's line of "it's a stick up stick up and a pick up pick up" is originally rapped as "big up, big up, it's a stick up, stick up" by Biggie, who tells a prospective victim that he'll be shot if he utters so much as a hiccup. It's a tense, hair-triggered moment that could easily turn fatal. Biggie is proclaiming himself "the opposite of peace," a force to be reckoned with in this world of transactional, almost banal violence. Cindi, having swapped the clauses, seems to want to transcend, rather than dominate, this world, but that goal will be difficult to accomplish. The danger is ever-present.

The appeal to gangster rap sensibilities is well calculated, casting androids as a criminalized underclass without access to the resources that would keep them out of harm's way.[3] In her seminal 2010 work *The New Jim Crow*, author and civil rights advocate Michelle Alexander describes the criminal justice system as a gateway into a "much larger system of racial stigmatization and permanent marginalization," a system that is impossible to escape once one has been ensnared. Alexander writes of denying criminals the right to the vote, to education, to employment, and to food stamps and other public benefits as a "stunningly comprehensive and well-designed system of racialized social control," creating a "growing undercaste, permanently locked up and locked out of mainstream society."

According to Alexander, there has been little social change since the collapse of Jim Crow, the segregationist set of laws enacted in the nineteenth and twentieth centuries. Instead, the change has come in the form of the language used to justify those laws:

> In the era of colorblindness, it is no longer socially permissible to use race, explicitly, as a justification for discrimination, exclusion, and social contempt. So we

[3] To further cement the connection the liner notes include, as inspirations for "Dance or Die," Brazilian drug lord Li'l Zé from the film *City of God*, and "Fela's cigarettes," in reference to Nigerian icon Fela Anikulapo Kuti, often outspoken against government authoritarianism and corruption both in and outside of his music, and often jailed as a result.

don't. Rather than rely on race, we use our criminal justice system to label people of color "criminals" and then engage in all the practices we supposedly left behind. . . . As a criminal, you have scarcely more rights, and arguably less respect, than a black man living in Alabama at the height of Jim Crow. We have not ended racial caste in America; we have merely redesigned it.

By aligning Metropolis's most maligned inhabitants with an over-criminalized subset of the American people permanently locked into a second-class citizenship, Monáe is creating an environment much like our own, where oppression is systemic, a faceless force that approaches from all sides.

It is notable that Cindi's story lacks a discernible antagonist. There may be bounty hunters, or Wolfmasters, or the people eager to see Cindi fall in "Tightrope," but Metropolis is not hostile to Cindi because of one evil overlord. There is no one tyrant whose defeat will bring peace. The injustice of Metropolis is institutional; the "Great Divide" that exists does so independently of individual acts of hatred. Instead, hatred is informed and enabled by this institutional injustice—the set of laws and conventions that would see androids kept permanently downtrodden. It is a Cold War, one that must be fought in the long term using as many different tactics as possible. Indeed in the song "Cold War," released as the album's second official single (though on the same day as "Tightrope"), that fight is made explicit.

"So you think I'm alone? / But being alone's the only way to be," sings Monáe, her clear-as-day vocals following ringing melody in a song that will not be overlooked. "Cold War" establishes an omnipresent matrix of control in which intimacy and connection are impossible, and a relocation "below the ground" is the only way to gain freedom. Cindi and her fellow androids spend their lives fighting for their very sanity, desperately trying to orient themselves in a world where they have been taught that something is wrong with them, that they are deserving of mistreatment.

This war is one that permeates every aspect of life in Metropolis, so much so that it can very quickly become a given, seen as an unremarkable and therefore unchangeable backdrop to the city. When Cindi sings, voice almost echoing from the grandness of her message, "Do you know what you're fighting for?" the answer is not an automatic yes. Though it may be difficult to visualize the sweeping systemic change needed to make Metropolis a more equitable place, that imaginative work is crucial. If any of us are to survive, we had "better know what [we]'re fighting for." Justice will prevail only if the weak are given wings, the strong given grace, and evil made to "stumble as it flies in the world." Cindi might sing of the need to "brave this night," but there will be many such nights before the world is changed for the better. So much is needed to ultimately defeat the system of surveillance, violence, instability, and repression that both Khan-Cullors and Alexander have spent their careers challenging.

In the music video for "Cold War," all embellishments have been removed. Monáe stands in extreme close-up, sound muted as she talks to someone off camera. She removes a robe, entirely unadorned save for a dramatic starburst of eyelashes. What follows is a single, uninterrupted take, the camera never straying from Monáe's face as she sings along to a song that is so clearly personal. The emotion keeps building, until suddenly, during the third verse, as Monáe reaches the lines "I'm trying to find my peace / I was made to believe there's something wrong with me / And it hurts my heart / Lord have mercy," she is overwhelmed. Tears well up in her eyes, and she stops singing, fighting to get back her control. As she reaches the climax of the song—the wordless, pained wails of someone so beaten and disheartened—a single tear has made it down her face, its track already drying.

The video, initially intended as something quite different, a more narratively focused project that would provide insight into the ArchAndroid mythos, is the final confirmation that what Monáe is singing about has not only happened to Cindi. There are real, barely healed wounds beneath the fantastical embellishments of the *ArchAndroid*'s story, wounds that Monáe feels keenly. Filmed after "Tightrope," during the last afternoon of a two-day shoot, the "Cold War" music video remains one of the most emotionally charged things director Wendy Morgan has ever experienced:

> We get into this little, intimate studio and there's so much love in the room because we've all been through the "Tightrope" experience all together. The very first take we do is this close up of Janelle and she starts to sing and she starts to cry and it's just so intense that everyone in the room started to cry. She sang the whole song and it was all legit, there was no acting in that. It was really just raw emotion.

The team continued, shooting almost an entire other video before, according to Morgan, deciding during the editing phase that "well this is the video, that's it."

This is the pain and doubt that everything has led up to. All of Cindi's world—the characters, the locales, the journey—has been in service of telling this story. The painfully unfiltered feeling of "Cold War" is the emotional crux of *The ArchAndroid*. When speaking of "Cold War" to *Rap-Up* magazine in 2010, Monáe makes clear that with the song, "you're in my mind and you get a chance to understand Metropolis, where it all stemmed [from]." In an iTunes LP interview, Lightning says that at one point the song was set to start off the album. "We always thought that it was kind of like a calling card, you set everyone in the right mood for the album, what was taking place on the whole album." The entirety of the struggle between love and doubt that has played out throughout *The ArchAndroid* is distilled in "Cold War." Though Monáe performed the song at the 2011 Nobel Peace Prize ceremony, make no mistake, "Cold War" was always, according to Wonder in the same iTunes LP interview, meant to "make you feel like you were going to war." Adds Lightning: "The music is a flag, and you're waving it."

Speaking to Khan-Cullors many years after the release of "Cold War," Monáe's fighting spirit is still intact. "We are in a rerouting, we are in an uprooting, we are in the midst of change," she says, full of the same brimming passion. "It's the power that we hold that is being held from us. We need to take it."

* * *

It is impossible to fully make sense of the many iterations of the android metaphor that Monáe deploys without understanding the many intersecting identities it is standing in for. Though the tribute to Black Lives Matter and the struggle against white supremacy is clear, what the android—as marginalized cyborg figure—represents is less a one-to-one parallel than an array of symbolic meanings that are able to shed light on just as many experiences of oppression. The android is "a new form of the Other," says Monáe to *Vice* in 2013. "Someone we can parallel the Other to: African-Americans, women, gays, lesbians, immigrants, and so on and so on. The minority . . . the one that does not have equal rights as [a] normal human being."[4] She would say something similar when speaking to Jenna Wortham in the *New York Times Magazine* in 2018. Cindi in particular, according to Wortham, is "a proxy for all the things about Monáe that made others uncomfortable, like her androgyny, her opaque sexual identity, her gender fluidity—her defiance of easy categorization."

When Kevin Barnes speaks about Of Montreal's relationship to the artists of Wondaland, particularly their collaborations during the summer of 2009 when the productions of their respective albums *False Priest* and *The ArchAndroid* took place,[5] he's quick to point to their shared

---

[4] In fact, the title of the 2013 single "Q.U.E.E.N." is an acronym for queer, untouchable, emigrant, excommunicated, and negroid, according to a 2013 fuse.tv interview, with Monáe stating that the song is for "everyone who's felt ostracized."

[5] That summer is commemorated in the liner notes of "Make the Bus" as the "Sunlandic Summer," in honor of Barnes's own fantasy world Sunlandia.

desire to build new worlds. "We both have these deep, rich fantasy worlds that we've created to exist inside of and allow other people to exist inside of." For Barnes, the drive to create such a place stems from "an unhappiness [with] the regular reality that you're forced to live in, or that you're expected to live in. Being dissatisfied with that reality and wanting to create something that is more fulfilling and feels more engaging and more positive."

The desire for a world more affirming to one's being seems to come from Monáe's own experiences as Black, as a woman, as pansexual and gender non-conforming. It's an intricate, layered understanding of identity and belonging best described by the term intersectionality, first introduced in 1989 by Kimberlé Williams Crenshaw in her landmark essay "Demarginalizing the Intersection of Race and Sex." A framework for understanding how various social and political identities come together to create unique experiences of oppression and privilege, intersectionality allows the cyborg metaphor to expand in any direction necessary.

Looking at Black women's place at the intersection of race and gender, and how those experiences are never addressed by political movements focused only on feminist or anti-racist concerns, Crenshaw writes of the dilemma caused by "ideological political currents that combine first to create and then to bury Black women's experiences." Separated, political work against racism or misogyny will always leave out those who are affected by more than one form of oppression, failing to take into account the needs of those affected by more than a single issue. "An analysis that does not take intersectionality into account," writes Crenshaw, "cannot sufficiently address the particular manner in which Black women are subordinated," and her point holds true no matter which political intersection is at hand.

Monáe, writing and singing from a multifaceted position in which she is acquainted with racialized violence and gender and sexuality-based subjugation, builds into her android an appeal to intersectionality that cannot be lifted out. Speaking to *Variety* in 2020, she says:

> I feel my feminine, I feel my masculine, I feel energy that I can't really explain. . . . I definitely don't live my life in a binary way. I've always pushed, as you can see from the way that I dress to the things that I've said since the beginning of my career. I've always fought against gender norms, and what it means to be a woman and what it means to be a man. I'm a fucking android.

And if Monáe was not, in 2010, open about her sexuality—the later *Dirty Computer* effectively functioning as her coming out album—the ways in which gender and sexuality have, from the earliest moments of her career, informed her kind of android are clear.

The very basic premise of *The ArchAndroid*—that of a criminalized love that disrupts all social convention—is queer. There is no way to remove queer analysis from the story of an outsider hunted and despised for how she chooses to love, though implications of class divide and miscegenation are certainly there as well. Beyond its single mention of Blueberry Mary in "Mushrooms & Roses," the entire project of *The ArchAndroid*, the love the album so ardently champions, corresponds to real-world forms of love that are still considered non-normative or threatening.

"There is a certain departure from the human that takes place in order to start the process of remaking the human," writes gender theorist Judith Butler in their work *Undoing Gender*. If the goal is to redefine the human, expanding its meaning so that all those who have historically been denied human rights can have access to the well-being and security those rights confer, it is necessary to explore the inhuman, what has previously been considered outside of the human. By acknowledging that "the terms by which we are recognized as human are socially articulated and changeable," as Butler does, it then becomes possible to look at the inhuman (the android), what it has represented (Blackness, queerness), and seek to remake the category of human into a more inclusive, affirming space.

The realm of the inhuman, that boundary so perfectly inhabited by the cyborg or android, is then fertile ground for much-needed political work, what José Esteban Muñoz terms the "necessary queer labor of the incommensurate."[6] Thinking outside of the regime of the human might be difficult work, but through such thinking much can be accomplished. By looking to Cindi and the revolution she is starting, the world she is trying to create for herself, we have a chance to bring progress to our own world well. Introducing Kesha and her performance of her triumphant survivor's anthem "Praying"

[6] "Theorizing Queer Inhumanisms: The Sense of Brownness."

at the 2018 Grammys, Monáe put all of that otherworldliness, all of that inhumanity, to powerful use. "We come in peace," she said, "but we mean business." The aliens, the androids, the monsters are here and ready to remake the world.

*   *   *

The love that Cindi feels is boundary shattering. Much like the love that would take center stage during the next decade of queer activism—marriage equality in many ways becoming the defining LGBTQIA+ rights fight of the 2010s—what Cindi feels is transformative, essential. When Monáe would officially come out in 2018, she would do so as a "free-ass motherfucker," perhaps knowing that queerness is not a shameful secret, ruefully admitted. It need not be an inconvenient truth for those with no choice but to be born this way. Queerness is freeing, love is freedom, and through Cindi—a tuxedo-clad being experiencing something far more complex, far less binary, than her programming anticipated—we see that freedom in action.

By wielding this power that defies categorization, that persists even in the face of criminalization, that despite moments of doubt believes in its own rightness, Cindi becomes the ArchAndroid. She becomes a leader among cyborgs, their chief and their exemplar. Her love is wild in "Faster," orgiastic in "Mushrooms & Roses," heartrendingly earnest in "Neon Valley Street," and is, as brown writes in *Pleasure Activism*, "the point. Feeling good is not frivolous, it is freedom." There is such potent political power in no longer feeling shame, in refusing to believe for one second more that you are broken and unworthy. "Find the pleasure in your life and follow it," urges brown. "Let it reverberate healing back into your ancestors' wounds. Let it open you up and remind you that you are already whole. Let it shape a future where feeling good is the normal, primary experience of all beings." Let the ArchAndroid guide the way.

In his work *They Can't Kill Us Until They Kill Us*, cultural critic Hanif Abdurraqib writes that artists of color make their best work when they make "music facing [their] people while also leaving the door open for everyone else to try and work their way in." He calls it freedom, this ability to "turn your eye back on the community you love and articulate it for an entire world that may not understand it as you do," and it is freedom because it is the artist who controls the language, controls the message, is able to bypass the "forces looking to control and commodify." Metropolis is a reflection of Monáe's world, a tribute to the obstacles that can so often be found blocking the lives of her audience, her people, and a tribute to their strength as well.

At its best, speculative fiction not only builds worlds, it offers alternative ways of being in these new worlds. The deep dissatisfaction with which Barnes has diagnosed both himself and Monáe, the feeling that leads to the creation of fantasy worlds, is a political response to injustice, a deep urge to create something more beautiful and fulfilling than what is already on offer. "It's kind of exceptional when an artist or an art collective operates on that level," he says, and he is not wrong. It is through these worlds that we are taught all that can yet be accomplished. "Fantasy is not the opposite of reality," writes Butler, "it is what reality forecloses, and, as a result, it defines the limits of reality"—limits that can then be stretched or entirely redrawn.

It is in speaking of the future that we give ourselves a chance to get it right. Metropolis is a world built to be transcended, a dangerous, cruel future explicitly constructed to be fallible. Cindi can free Metropolis, can triumph over the Great Divide, and in so doing act as guide for listeners as they seek to transcend the limits of their own world. "Because we have learned to believe negativity is more realistic," writes bell hooks in *All About Love*, "it appears more real than any positive voice. Once we begin to replace negative thinking with positive thinking, it becomes utterly clear that, far from being realistic, negative thinking is absolutely disenabling." The surface of Cindi's story may be fantastical, but its core, that love that can survive the worst despair, is real. It cannot be lost; it must be believed in.

The ArchAndroid's penultimate song "Say You'll Go" inspires that belief. A multi-faith paean with all the romance of Stevie Wonder's "Girl Blue" (a liner note inspiration with clear musical ties), the song offers salvation through a love so pure it will last past destruction and death. Cindi's love "is not a fantasy," but it is still rare, "a place few people go or ever know." Cindi urges us to find the courage to face the release of Nirvana, asking if we are brave enough to "leave Samsara," or the cyclical, constantly reincarnating world, and instead reach enlightenment, "find forever" in an eternal love.

Inspired, according to the liner notes, by the Exodus, "Say You'll Go" offers a liberation akin to the Israelites leaving Egypt and their bondage behind. In another biblical turn, we are invited to "witness the interaction of / The flood, the sea, the sky, the dove," assured that "time erodes the shore but not our love." This love is steadfast, everlasting, and even if the world were to end, it would "sail in this ark" forever. It is a beautiful surrender, the watery instrumentation giving way to piano and vocals, nearly two minutes of bliss set to Debussy's "Clair de lune."

This is the way forward for Cindi, a path of divine love, of righteous love, the love she has found with Anthony and in Wondaland. This is how she will make her world better, how Metropolis can be righted of its wrongs. Chuck Lightning, speaking at a 2016 Moogfest panel, articulates it best:

> We do tell stories at Wondaland that are dystopian in nature, but we are real optimists. We really do believe in the human spirit and our ability to continue to liberate ourselves and emancipate others. Even though there may be darkness—even in the music sometimes there's darkness—there's always something in there, there's always a ray of light, there's always some magic. If you go to the point right where the song is fading out, you hear one note or one melody come in, that'll just take your mind away to something else. I think those are those little moments that we're fighting for.

There is so much darkness in Metropolis, and so much darkness in our own world. But if we focus on our loves and our desire for a better world for those we love, we just might be able to harness a little bit of Cindi's magic, a little bit of her power. We can find, like Cindi and like Monáe, survival through music, through love, through Wondaland.

5
Wondaland

If you want something, you had better make some noise.
—*Malcolm X*[1]

"I honestly feel I haven't even tapped 25% of my potential for what I can do and what I can be," says Monáe to the *Guardian* in 2014, a statement that was certainly true with the advent of *The ArchAndroid*'s release. A month after its May release, the album would peak at #17 on the Billboard 200, staying on the list for another sixteen weeks before dropping off in October.[2] Certainly a much better showing than the reissued *Metropolis*'s one-week stint at #115, but less high-reaching than either *Electric Lady* or *Dirty Computer*—charting for

[1] *The Autobiography of Malcolm X*. Copyright © 1964 by Alex Healey and Malcolm X, copyright © 1965 by Alex Healey and Betty Shabazz. Published by Penguin Books 1965, Hutchinson 1966, Penguin Books 1968, Penguin Classics 2001. Used with permission from Penguin Books Ltd and Penguin Random House LLC.

[2] *The ArchAndroid* would also spend forty-four weeks on the Top R&B/Hip-Hop Albums chart, topping out at number four.

sixteen and eight weeks apiece, and peaking at #5 and #6 respectively—would turn out to be. There was much Monáe could yet accomplish.

Everything about *The ArchAndroid*, from its highflying concept to its genre bending musical stylings, shows an unwillingness to compromise or comply with the demands of the 2010 pop market. Though concessions were surely made—Lightning telling me that Monáe's career was essentially built out of a "master class" strategy conversation between Sean Combs and Atlantic Records' Julie Greenwald—the album feels rooted in artistry in a way that seems decidedly at odds with the most commercially successful music of the day. Despite massive critical success for the album, including Grammy nominations for *The ArchAndroid* and "Tightrope," even the ambassadorial single couldn't quite mesh with the year's established tone. As demonstrated by its top singles, 2010 was a year of both saccharine sentimentality (Train's "Hey, Soul Sister" and "Need You Now" by the band formerly known as Lady Antebellum) and a deep and abiding silliness ("Tik Tok," "California Gurls," and the Usher/will.i.am joint "OMG," a song I will never, ever forgive for the lyrics "honey got some boobies like wow oh wow"). It would take several years before a more ambitious poptimism would change the music landscape and catch up with what Monáe was doing.

But knowing what she was doing, and the clarity that that singular focus offered, would prove very beneficial for Monáe over the course of the next decade. Musically, she would continue to tell Cindi Mayweather's story with 2013's *Electric Lady*, and branch out into a more personal direction with *Dirty Computer* in 2018. She would collaborate with

Solange, Erykah Badu, Stevie Wonder, Prince, Pharrel, Brian Wilson, Esperanza Spalding, and more. She would tour each of her own albums and headline a 2015 tour designed to promote the Wondaland-released *The Eephus*—an EP that brought together Wondaland acts Jidenna, St. Beauty, Roman GianArthur, and Deep Cotton.

She would tour with Of Montreal in 2010, and with Bruno Mars, Fun, and Amy Winehouse in 2011. She would also open for Erykah Badu and Katy Perry in 2011 and take part in dozens of festivals over the years, including Coachella, Afropunk, Bonnaroo, SXSW, and Lilith Fair. She would perform at the White House on two occasions and open the 2020 Oscars with an adapted version of "Come Alive." At the 2010 BET Awards she would perform Prince's "Let's Go Crazy," and in 2016 she would return to that stage to sing a medley of Prince's songs in a tribute to the recently deceased icon and mentor.

Wanting to act as well, Monáe turned down nearly thirty movie offers before taking a role in the Oscar-winning *Moonlight* in 2016, the same year she would also appear in *Hidden Figures* as NASA engineer Mary Jackson. Monáe played a customer service AI in the *Philip K. Dick's Electric Dreams* episode "Autofac" in 2017, and a friend and mentor to Harriet Tubman in 2019's *Harriet*. In 2020, she appeared in *The Glorias*, the second season of *Homecoming*, and *Antebellum*. Describing *Antebellum*, a film with its own Afrofuturist project, Monáe said in an Instagram Live interview with Patrisse Khan-Cullors, "this is a film that connects the dots between the past, the present, and the future and what it can look like." An extension of her own work as herself and as Cindi Mayweather, Monáe's roles span centuries, taking us from Antebellum South to unknowable distant future.

In whatever spare time all this allowed, Monáe also became a darling of the fashion world. Though the black-and-white color palette largely remained, the tuxedo uniform slowly expanded to include looks by the likes of Chanel, Vivienne Westwood, Balmain, Ralph Lauren, and more, worn at Met Galas, Paris Fashion Weeks, and red carpet after red carpet.

Her advocacy work, too, would readily take center stage. In addition to the 2015 release of "Hell You Talmbout," Monáe was one of the original signatories for the Time's Up open letter in 2018, a document from women working in film, television, and theater calling for an end to sexual assault and harassment. She became an ambassador for the Alicia Keys-founded Keep a Child Alive, an organization committed to combating the impacts of HIV/AIDS, and recorded "This Is for My Girls" with Missy Elliott, Kelly Clarkson, Zendaya, and others in support of the Michelle Obama campaigns Let Girls Learn and #62milliongirls.

In 2020 she would fight Covid-19-caused food insecurity with #WondaLunch, a two-city, drive-through free lunch and voter registration initiative. In partnership with the nonprofit Project Isaiah, Wondalunch hired out of work airport catering employees to put together thousands of lunches for whoever might be in need. Monáe would also call for justice for the murder of George Floyd, and publicly donate to the Minnesota Freedom Fund. In anticipation of the 2020 election, she would release the song and short film "Turntables" for Stacey Abram's documentary *All In:*

The Fight for Democracy. Unafraid to turn her principles into action, Monáe would spend years, like she says in "Turntables," keeping her "hands dirty [but her] mind clean."

"One of my biggest strengths is I'm unafraid to say no," Monáe told *Fast Company* in 2018. "I'm not into people owning me. I have a strong vision, and any companies or partners who want to work with me have to match my purpose: shaping culture, redefining culture, and moving culture forward." And the ability to say no was one she used frequently early in her career, as she told Roxane Gay in 2020 for *The Cut*: "That was my secret weapon. Once I started to eliminate the things that didn't feel in line with where I was trying to go, and that could potentially pigeonhole me from having that freedom as an artist, it was very helpful."

Monáe's career—the achievements listed here are only the highlights of an even more robust résumé—is proof positive that there is much that Monáe wants to say yes to, and that she has the drive and commitment to turn those dreams into reality. As she told the *Guardian* in 2014: "It's true. I am part-android . . . I am rewarded with singularity. My mind works at an exponential rate." Hers is an astounding work ethic, one that many attribute to her inspiration, James "hardest working man in show business" Brown, but one that Monáe is quick to thank her mother for. Her breakneck pace makes the five years between *Electric Lady* and *Dirty Computer* all the more noticeable, a length of time that would not have stretched so long had it not been for the loss of close friend and advisor Prince. "This was the person that I would literally call and talk to about sounds or 'How should I say this? Is this saying too much?' " Monáe would tell the *New York Times*

Magazine in 2018. "I just never could imagine a time where I couldn't pick up the phone or email him, and he'd contact me right back and we'd talk about all these things that I was unsure of." The loss of Prince's friendship and mentorship was profound, the only thing, it seems, that could possibly slow Monáe down.

Prince's legacy, however, lives on in much of Monáe's work, particularly in the creation of Wondaland, Monáe's Atlanta-based arts society. Though inspired by the Harlem Renaissance, Andy Warhol's Factory, the Black Arts Movement, and George Clinton's Mothership, Wondaland owes much to Prince's production complex and home Paisley Park. "If there was no Paisley Park," Monáe said at Moogfest 2016, "nine times out of ten Wondaland wouldn't have the blueprint to remain a creative movement." The business aspect in particular is critical to Wondaland's success, adds Lightning: "One of the central tenets of Wondaland is that it's important for people of color not to just be consumers but to be owners and producers. Not to just be the object but something more, the subject." For Wondaland to remain a creative force, it also must hold corporate sway. "We always talk about our lawyer being the genesis of Wondaland," says Lightning. "We were jamming before, but when we got an attorney we really started jamming. We're very serious about that."

Housed in a large but unassuming residential Atlanta home with instruments stashed in corners and hanging off walls, Wondaland is headed by a Vision Board of Monáe, Wonder, and Lightning, and is comprised of ten or so employees—all with fluid job descriptions and who pitch in where needed. "We're all involved in the music side and the film side and the endorsement side and the activism side," Monáe told *Fast Company* in 2018, and for all the importance of Wondaland acting as a company, it is all in service to art and revolution. "Wondaland is my creative oasis. It's full of artists, full of filmmakers, musicians, visual artists. A collective that really does want to redefine what it means to create, to give. It's a place for those who want to shake up the world."[3]

A "school for mutants and droids," Wondaland offers space for young creatives to gather, learn, and "piss off the Old Guard of gatekeepers who don't understand the value of [B]lack-renaissance artists," says Monáe.[4] A house where one is as likely to stumble onto a book club or communal meal as a jam session, Wondaland offers the space and resources needed for a variety of artists and thinkers to thrive. The cast of the Afrofuturist blockbuster *Black Panther* held impromptu gatherings at Wondaland during filming, surely recognizing the society as a place of kindred spirits. "When we come to Wondaland we'll read, sometimes we'll be in the studio creating music, we rehearse, have dialogue . . . everything," says Alex Belle, one half of the duo St. Beauty.[5] Wondaland's purpose is thus to fulfil both material and artistic needs, with Belle's band mate Isis Valentino describing it as "just the space for orphans to come."[6]

[3] Westenberg, Emma. "Janelle Monáe—A Revolution of Love (Artist Spotlight Stories)," YouTube Music, 2018.

[4] Gay, Roxane. "Janelle Monáe's Afrofuture: 'It Looks Like an Orgasm and the Big Bang While Skydiving as Grace Jones Smiles,'" *The Cut*, 2020.

[5] Westenberg.

[6] Ibid.

There's freedom to be found in Wondaland, and its namesake song on *The ArchAndroid* says as much. A crossroads for lost people who nevertheless are in possession of grand artistic visions, Wondaland does indeed function as a space "where dreamers meet" and magic minds make love to one another. The "Wondaland" of song is a place where the "grass grows inside," and where music will float "you gently on your toes" while changing your "clothes to tuxedos." Fantastical details, to be sure, but ones that have real-life corollaries in the tuxedo uniforms often donned by many of the society's core members, and the turf laid out in the Wondaland house. Even the brick-and-mortar Wondaland is a fantasy world, decorated with dense palm trees, tropical fish in aquariums lit with purple light, and a wall of contradictory clocks (for the time travelers).

But more than a physical space, Wondaland is an ethos, one committed to helping people, "encouraging them to be the best them that they can be and embracing their unique qualities and using them as superpowers," said Monáe to the *Current* in 2010, before adding, "and we also make capes for superheroes in the winter." It is a fitting metaphor for a collective whose goal is both to empower and to protect, to create space for artistry to flourish while also counteracting the disadvantages that would cause that artistry to go untapped. At Moogfest 2016, Wonder paraphrases the lyrics of "Cold War" when describing the collective's goal, stating Wondaland's founding words as "providing for those that don't have, giving wings to [the] ideas of those who cannot bring wings to them themselves." It is an ethos of care that makes Wondaland a "pay it forward kind of place," according to Monáe, who adds, "and I love that. I love that we're realizing that we're stronger together. That we can shape culture in a very positive way, in a cool-ass way, if we stick together."[7]

During the Wondaland panel at Moogfest 2016, Monáe would again articulate the importance of nurturing the Black creativity around her:

> We kind of created our own Afrotopia, where we saw a world where artists could just be artists, poets could be poets, coders could code. We had actors, we had painters, we had all these people who had these ideas, and we wanted to make sure we were cultivating, helping cultivate, helping fertilize those ideas. Because ideas help shape and change the world as we know it.

That cultivation does indeed produce fertile ground for collaboration, another core component of how Wondaland operates. At every step, Wondaland seems committed to pushing forward the careers of all its members, whether through Monáe taking St. Beauty on tour with her after *Dirty Computer*'s release, or using her celebrity to promote other Wondaland artists on *The Eephus*, an EP instrumental in launching Jidenna's career.

Monáe's film and television contracts now stipulate that she or other Wondaland members will be involved with the music. Which explains how Jidenna's song "Classic Man," performed with GianArthur, can be heard in *Moonlight*. When Monáe voiced the Peggy Lee pound dog in 2019's *Lady and the Tramp*,

[7] Ibid.

Wonder and GianArthur came with, writing additional music and voicing a pair of troublemaking cats. In Monáe's star vehicle *Antebellum*, Wonder and GianArthur composed the score. The members of Wondaland, many of whom have been with Monáe from the earliest days of her career, are a family, committed to succeeding as one. It is clear what these relationships mean to Monáe, as both friendships and professional partnerships. Early in her *Electric Lady* acknowledgments, she thanks the entirety of the Wondaland Arts Society "for being my family. My nucleus," adding, "You are the consummate Artists, Lovers, Thought Leaders, Visionaries, Dreamers, Imaginateers, Thrivals, Fighters, Forgivers, and true Givers of the future. I'm honored I W.A.S. here with you."

That closeness is evident to all those who come into contact with Wondaland, it seems. "The truth is they really, truly work like a collective," says Wendy Morgan of Monáe, Wonder, and Lightning. Production designer Jessee Clarkson agrees, telling me that "everybody in there, the people, Janelle's creative team, were her family." Clarkson, who built both the Metropolis crown on the cover of *The ArchAndroid* and the masks for the "Tightrope" mirror-faces, adds that "the people that she surrounds herself with are all very much on the same page, and very collaborative." Though it was at first daunting to work with such a large group of decision makers, since "from [the perspective of] a fabricator working in the film industry, when you do that you get thirty different opinions," that wasn't his experience of Wondaland. "Everybody was really included in the process, on the same team and open to ideas."

It's a working relationship Morgan also experienced, telling me that the team was "involved with the creative more so than a normal artist and their people. A lot more." But with that came an unexpected clarity of vision. "I was just kind of a conduit," says Morgan, "directing this music video with a lot of their ideas." Though perhaps not quite a science fictional hive mind, Wondaland does present an interesting example of professional and creative unity, one possible only after years of relationship building. "It seems like something that she treasures," says Kevin Barnes of Monáe's tendency to keep Wondaland members close, adding, "once you earn her respect and her love, you have it forever." And for Morgan, the feeling is mutual: "I have nothing but love for those people."

Wondaland is the theory and the practice, the dream that has been dreamt and can now be lived in. The belief system that the ArchAndroid espouses, a belief in love and in power that comes from care and community, is enacted in how Wondaland operates. In "Locked Inside," Cindi sings of "the writers and the artists . . . paid to tell us lies / To keep us locked inside." But once those same artists have visited Wondaland, have been allowed the space to create outside of the tyrannical regime of the Great Divide, "the golden door of their emotions opens wide / Here they fall into their love and never have to hide."[8] Wondaland, the fact and the fiction of it, ensures that art has a chance to live in this world, and that once they have been dreamt, "these dreams are forever."[9]

* * *

[8] "Mushrooms & Roses."
[9] "Dance or Die."

The initial plan for *The ArchAndroid* was to create a full "emotion picture" titled *Dance or Die*. It would have been a cohesive visual album years before Beyoncé would fully bring the form into the mainstream with *Beyoncé* and *Lemonade*. And while it was not to be for *The ArchAndroid*, that plan would come to fruition for *Dirty Computer*, whose accompanying film features the character of Jane 57821—acting as a sort of psychic middle ground between Monáe and Cindi—who must fight for her right to remain a dirty computer, to remain unique in who she is. The idea for a cinematic accompaniment was always there, the perfect way to convey ideas too big for any one medium. Stretching even as far back as Monáe's first music video, the robot slave auction cum fashion show of "Many Moons," each video was always meant to be part of a larger film. Over a decade later, in her acknowledgments in the *Dirty Computer* liner notes, Monáe would thank Lightning for "making [her] emotion picture dreams come true," adding: "We made a movie man! Now let's eat some popcorn and watch this rebel music unfold across the world."

Cindi's story was also meant to live on in graphic novel form as *The Red Book*, fleshing out the story of the ArchAndroid and providing context for the album. *ArchAndroid* concept artist Chad Weatherford had even begun producing thumbnails for a Lightning-penned script, with the original plan of illustrating the first five issues himself before handing off the reins. Though these plans would take a back seat as well, Weatherford says that Lightning, in particular, still talks about the project.

The advent of *Electric Lady* brought a much-needed new chapter of Cindi's story, one that, in true time traveler fashion, sometimes seems like a prequel to the *Metropolis* EP (placed in a time before Anthony Greendown) and sometimes seems like Cindi's next step, a portrait of a messiah coming into her power and changing the political landscape of Metropolis through song. "I like to think you can hear me using my superpowers this time," says Monáe in a website bio around the time *Electric Lady*'s release. "And not just talking or wondering about them." Though the ArchAndroid saga was initially conceived of as four suites, once *Electric Lady* was released it became clear that future installments would be necessary, with seven suites now anticipated. *Electric Lady*, continues Monáe, is "like the big action sequence in the third act of an epic film." Fittingly, as it stands the best chance of resuming Cindi's story post–*Electric Lady* will likely be through film. In 2018, Wondaland signed a film development deal with Universal, and, given Monáe's penchant for multimedia storytelling, it seems like *The ArchAndroid* might come to life on the big screen— Weatherford, at least, has been busy producing images for the pitch.

The sky is the limit for Monáe, this twenty-eighth-century being for whom "there's never going to be enough,"[10] and it's impossible to tell what might come next. But whatever new projects are on the horizon for Monáe and for Wondaland, they will undoubtedly be strategic. Wondaland is tightly knit, but also tightly controlled. "They have this real mystery that they had created, and they were kind of protective of it," says

---

[10] Ringen, Jonathan. "How Singer-Songwriter, Actress-Activist Janelle Monáe Gets So Much Done," *Fast Company*, 2018.

Morgan. "Janelle too, there's a mystery to her. She doesn't show that much of her[self]." The mythos of Wondaland, of Janelle Monáe, is strong. The same beats, the same stories, come up again and again, in past interviews and in anecdotes told by collaborators. Monáe's style and its roots, the unified vision of Cindi's story, the ironclad collaborative relationship between the core Wondaland crew, it all seems to have emerged fully formed. For the casual viewer there's almost no trace of evolution, or refinement. Cindi might as well be Monáe's Athena, striding into the world fully formed with pristine saddle shoes and a mission to save the world. For art that manages to mean so many things to so many people, the media messaging behind the artist is surprisingly cohesive.

At every stage of her career, the stories are all the same. Even when they seem spontaneous, unplanned, dig deep enough into the Janelle Monáe Media Narrative and only patterns emerge. In a 2013 cover story for *Pitchfork*, Carrie Battan writes that Monáe's disclosure about finding the title Electric Lady in therapy seems "blurted out, seemingly by accident," but the same nugget is featured prominently in other outlets. Dorian Lynskey, writing for the *Guardian* in 2010, makes particular mention of that control of expression, calling Monáe "possibly the most focused, self-contained person I have ever encountered. Her choice of words is as meticulous as her choice of outfit, which is to say extremely." The interview progresses, but for Lynskey there's "the distinct impression that she's given this speech before." Battan, too, eventually expresses a similar sentiment: "I often feel like she's speaking to me from a script, reflexively keeping emotional distance between us." Even as late as 2020, Roxane Gay, when profiling Monáe for *The Cut*, writes that "it's difficult to truly know" Monáe and "who and what she loves, what brings her true joy, what she most yearns for." There was real intimacy to their conversations, but only, says Gay, "within very specific boundaries."

Still, Monáe's public persona post-*Dirty Computer* is light-years from what it was earlier in her career. There's a lot separating the Monáe of 2010, telling *Rolling Stone* that she only dates androids ("Nothing like an android—they don't cheat on you"), and the Monáe of 2018 nervously, but resolutely, telling the same magazine that she has loved people of more than one gender. Monáe might have been mulling over *Dirty Computer* as an idea even before the release of *The ArchAndroid*, but it took the intervening years and a growing comfort in her own skin for the more personal album to finally emerge.

"I was really afraid for anybody to see me not at the top of my game," said Monáe to *Smithsonian Magazine* in 2018. It's a common theme in many of her media appearances the year of *Dirty Computer*'s release, that idea that Janelle Monáe was finally ready to open up. "I used to be a lot more afraid of going off script," she would tell the *New York Times Magazine*, worrying about her legacy and "the whole concept of what I'll be remembered for." It was an anxiety she was able to dodge as long as Cindi Mayweather buffered her from the world. "I created her, so I got to make her be whatever I wanted her to be," Monáe would tell *Rolling Stone* that same year. "I didn't have to talk about the Janelle Monáe who was in therapy." Cindi, fallible despite her awesome power, was allowed to be flawed. Allowed to be openly afraid when looking to the future and seeing "danger in its eyes."[11] Allowed to struggle and learn, make mistakes and strive to be better. But Monáe could not, it seems, extend herself that same grace. Despite her increasing success, the question remained: "What if people don't think I'm as interesting as Cindi Mayweather?"[12]

If the public didn't really know Janelle Monáe, that was fine. "I felt like I didn't really have to be her because they were fine with Cindi," said Monáe to the *New York Times Magazine*. "I knew I needed to make this album, and I put it off and put it off because the subject was Janelle Monáe." The lesson at the heart of *Dirty Computer*, of learning to love one's flaws, is well chosen. "For a while I was trying to clean myself, trying to make myself appear perfect," said Monáe to the *Smithsonian* magazine, before adding that now she "respect[s] the dirt. It's about the dirt and not getting rid of it." In *The Cut* in 2020, she would elaborate: "I was discovering more and more about my sexuality. I was walking into being more sex positive, also understanding different ways to love and to be loved. . . . *Dirty Computer* was really a reflection of where I was at that time."

Now that Monáe has been candid about herself like never before, has shucked the mantle of Cindi Mayweather (if only temporarily) and revealed herself to be brokenly, beautifully human after all, it's tempting to view Cindi as nothing more than armor, a smokescreen behind which to hide. And while that's certainly been a dominant media narrative, to believe

---

[11] "Locked Inside."

[12] Spanos, Brittany. "Janelle Monáe Frees Herself," *Rolling Stone*, 2018.

it would be misguided. We tell the stories we need to see in the world, and Monáe is no exception. "Cindi helps me talk more," she told the *New York Times Magazine* in 2018. A persona perfectly put together to channel her creator's music and ideas, Cindi is more figurehead than ventriloquist's dummy, and Monáe more collaborator than puppet master.

If with Metropolis she gives herself a framework through which to approach the problems of our own world, with Cindi Monáe allows herself the freedom to approach her own problems. Cindi's story works as laboratory, a space in which to experiment and learn. And Cindi herself is perfectly suited to accommodate the blurring of boundaries between story and storyteller. There is nothing better than a cyborg to occupy two spaces, two perspectives, at once. To view the android as misdirection is reductive, and if Monáe has seen fit to step beyond Cindi's scope, it is in service to her expansion as an artist. Though she would tell the *Guardian* in 2010 that "black and white keeps [her] centered rather than in a grey area," by 2018 those restrictions clearly mattered less: "There's so much grey. And I think I'm kind of discovering the grey and realising that it's OK not to have all the answers, or to supply them."[13] *Dirty Computer* is then an experiment not just in existing in the liminal spaces but of exploring endless possibilities and allowing herself "to use all the shades of the crayon box."[14]

[13] Bengal, Rebecca. "'You Don't Own or Control Me': Janelle Monáe on Her Music, Politics and Undefinable Sexuality," *Guardian*, 2018.
[14] Ibid.

That Monáe wishes to paint something other than Cindi "Electric Lady #1" Mayweather does nothing to discount the power of the ArchAndroid's story. Monáe herself has certainly never disavowed her past persona. She dedicated *Electric Lady* to Cindi, thanking the android in the liner notes for "coming into my dreams and my paintings. You sent me your songs, your thoughts, your prayers, your stories and through you I was able to activate myself. I wouldn't want to share DNA with anyone other than you. See you where I always see you, in the future." In *Rolling Stone* in 2018, she would describe her relationship with Cindi even more succinctly: "She is who I aspire to be." Cindi's story will return one day, that much is certain. There is still so much she can teach us all. But as our time with *The ArchAndroid* comes to a close, how are we to say goodbye to Cindi? What ending can possibly do justice to this story of a messiah who finds true love and her true purpose? What else but a love song.

*   *   *

"'BaBopByeYa' was actually started before I was born," says Roman GianArthur, the song's arranger and brother to Nate Wonder, in an iTunes LP interview. "It was a piece that was written originally by my father, Dr. Nathaniel Irvin II. He wrote the piece in 1976." The two brothers grew up with a song older than they were, listening as their father played it on the piano. Later, the cherished memory would be turned into something entirely new, though imbued with that same gentle wash of nostalgia.

In this version of "BaBopByeYa," menacing horns blare out as the piano of "Say You'll Go" fades from memory. Sounding off over twitchy percussion, the horns have a dangerous quality, a two-note progression much like the opening of the James Bond theme that remains unresolved, unsettled. It takes more than a minute of prowling instrumentation for Cindi to be found, but once she begins to sing it is with a voice that is the clearest it has been at any point in the album. While in *Pitchfork*'s review of *The ArchAndroid* Monáe is labeled a "vocal chameleon who places the needs of her songs ahead of her ego," in "BaBopByeYa" whatever lizard skin remains has been shed. This is Monáe at her most operatic, unleashing an epic vocal performance with all the yearning of "Neon Valley Street" and all the spiritual transcendence of "Say You'll Go." It is a bittersweet farewell, the album closing on Cindi as she is separated from her love, hearing "echoes of [his] laughter in the corners of [her] mind."

"She is calling out to Anthony Greendown, who is her BaBopByeYa," says Monáe in the same iTunes LP interview. "There's a special call for him, and a special call for her. And when they hear that, they immediately know that they're safe and everything's okay." This is perhaps again an allusion to Harriet Tubman, this time her ability to use owl calls as signals on the Underground Railroad, and the reference makes it clear that danger is still omnipresent. As Cindi sings to Anthony "they know all about you" and then "I will leave without you," it is separation borne out of necessity. Where Cindi Mayweather must go, Anthony Greendown cannot, for his own safety, follow.

A nearly nine-minute tour de force, "BaBopByeYa" dances from spy thriller to exquisite tango, with Monáe's desperate, belted vocals and unadorned spoken word communicating the entirety of her passion. From the sweetest whispered admission of love to the keening ache of loss, there is, as Wonder puts it: "a whole love story in the song"[15]—one that will live forever in the memory of its singer. "BaBopByeYa" is a monumental finale, bookending the grandness of *The ArchAndroid*'s overtures—also arranged by GianArthur—and acting as a fitting sendoff for Cindi as she ventures forward toward the unknown. Where or when she might be going, we can only guess, but this visionary who can "see beyond tomorrow" is needed in more than one place, and more than one time. How fitting that her last moments with us are communicated through a piece written by a man who was not yet a father, a song finished by the son. That, too, is time travel.

* * *

Given that the narrative post–Cindi Mayweather has been one of emancipation, one of freedom from self-imposed secrecy and artifice, I had hoped to speak frankly with Monáe herself about her first full-length album with the perspective and distance of the intervening decade. But apart from a few phone calls with Lightning, schedules did not line up and it was sadly not to be. Some things will have to remain a mystery, for as Monáe put it to the *Guardian* in 2013, "Does the world and everybody have all of me? No—even I don't have all of me. Janelle Monáe is evolving constantly, and she

---

[15] *The ArchAndroid* (Deluxe), iTunes LP, 2010.

is blossoming. You get the real me in real time—and that's as real as it's going to get." In the end I find I can't argue with that.

It is that sense of endless reinvention, after all, that makes Monáe able to keep changing and growing, an artist capable of making truly dynamic music. It is that versatility that can create *Electric Lady,* the "soundtrack for the Obama era" according to a website bio, and can respond to a much more dire political climate—"the first time I've felt threatened and unsafe as a young [B]lack woman, growing up in America"[16]— with *Dirty Computer* only a few short years later. "I am an artist who will not be any one thing to you, or to myself," she would tell the attendees of Moogfest 2016. "And I owe it to myself, and those who fought for my freedom, to be free. As much as I can."

That freedom is found and nurtured in Wondaland and the people who make the society what it is. In building a business tailored to her and her interests, Monáe has created the conditions for her continued success. "What you see at Wondaland, it's completely unique," says Morgan. "I'm in Atlanta and I'm surrounded by this young Black intelligentsia. Everyone is wearing black and white and tuxedos. They were living their lives as art. It wasn't just a project, it was much more than that, and I think it still is." Through Wondaland Monáe's work shines, impossible to ignore. "Almost right off the bat, she's singing with Patti LaBelle and Aretha Franklin," says Clarkson. "She's up there with the greats and

---

[16] Wortham, Jenna. "How Janelle Monáe Found Her Voice," *New York Times Magazine,* 2018.

deservedly so." When asked about his first impressions of Monáe, Barnes doesn't waste time with understatement. He describes her as "someone that was destined to take over the world, and destined to make the world a better place," before continuing:

> She has such positive energy and is such an incredible performer. The whole group—the whole band, the whole clique or whatever that they're a part of—was so focused and committed to what they were doing on a level that I've never seen before. Just the level of professionalism and attention to detail and focus that they have for everything that they're involved with. They never phone anything in. Every performance I've ever seen her give, it's been James Brown-level, Prince-level mastery. It's amazing to meet someone like that.

It is rare to find someone for whom these words—mastery, destiny—are so readily used by so many. Rarer still for those words to be so obviously appropriate.

Monáe and Cindi are not the same, that much is clear. The larger-than-life android shouldering the responsibility of an entire world is necessarily operating far outside the scope of any one person. We expect Monáe-the-artist to have imbued Cindi-the-art with her own feelings and aspirations, but there is also so much of Cindi's greatness in Monáe. There is so much of the ArchAndroid in how Monáe chooses to live and create publicly, in how she chose to respond to a worsening global political climate by living bigger and loving harder. That is Cindi's power, brought into our world. For Cindi and, it would appear, for Monáe, there is no question of retreating when met with hate. There is only the option of embracing love instead, of being more open, more visible, more free in that love. As quoted in her website bio around the time of *The ArchAndroid*'s release, Monáe says that through the album she means to encourage listeners to "embrace their own superpowers and become the voice of change, the hero—or The ArchAndroid—in their own communities." Cindi was never meant to be a shield, holding the world back from a more authentic Monáe. Cindi was always a harbinger of things to come, the symbol of a power available to all of us, Monáe included.

I don't question when people speak of Monáe as someone who will change the world, because as musician, as celebrity, and as icon, I think it's clear she already has. She is only human, it's true, but it's fitting that her work has stretched far beyond the human into the realm of the cyborg. Monáe's ideas could change everything, could upend everything we think we know about the world. Through Cindi we've seen what love and dedication can look like, and through Monáe we've seen how they can be applied. I believe Monáe when she says that what we have seen of her is only a quarter of what she is capable of. I believe that for all the worlds she has created, there is still more yet to come. I believe in the ArchAndroid, and I cannot wait to see what comes next.

BaBopByeYa
Conclusion

I didn't fall in love. I rose in it.
—*Toni Morrison*[1]

"From childhood on, I found many angels in favorite authors," writes bell hooks in *All About Love*, "writers who created books that enabled me to understand life with greater complexity. These works opened my heart to compassion, forgiveness, and understanding." For hooks, though angels need not always be religious figures, they nevertheless act as guides, leading us toward love and reminding us "that there is a realm of mystery that cannot be explained by human intellect or will." I've spent much of this book treating *The ArchAndroid* as a literary document, analyzing it less as a work of music and more as one would a piece of writing. The album works well under such parameters. There's a richness to the lyrics that allow them to work as text, even if the addition of the music creates a sophisticated prosody that provides layer upon layer of additional meaning. From the panicked flight of "Dance or Die" through to the self-possessed ascension of "BaBopByeYa," Cindi's story is for me that book that hooks describes. *The ArchAndroid* is that guide toward greater understanding.

In the bridge of "Dance or Die," Saul Williams utters a list of seemingly disjointed ideas. His spoken word becomes almost a chant, a ritual invocation of imagery that, upon closer inspection, offers a curious, understated synopsis of Cindi's journey on the album. Cindi is "gunshot, dodging," merely surviving Metropolis until she begins to "dream, bright." Only once she harnesses those dreams is she able to "beat" the Great Divide, "light" up Metropolis, and "breathe [and] live" free of fear. In order to "help, give," she'll need to become the ArchAndroid and step into her power—or, put differently, to "focus, trance, wake up, dance." At the outset of this trajectory, the word that begins Williams's catalog, the idea that best defines Cindi and her potential, is, fittingly, "angel." Cindi is the "love angel" of "Wondaland" and the voice that, according to hooks, "tell[s] us it is only by loving that we enter an earthly paradise." In choosing love, we are listening to angels. Their messages may come in the form of a book, or a song, but however they appear and whatever our individual circumstances may be, we can, according to hooks, "listen to the voices of hope that . . . tell us paradise is our home and love our true destiny."

Opening up to love is not easy. It can only happen once "we find ourselves in the right place at the right time, ready and able to receive blessings without knowing just how we got there," says hooks. "Often we look at events retrospectively and can trace a pattern, one that allows us to intuitively recognize the presence of an unseen spirit guiding and directing our path." And so it is with the story of the ArchAndroid, a fable I didn't realize had so affected me until the animating force behind it, Janelle Monáe, stepped outside of it.

*   *   *

It's early 2018 and I'm in the thick of a master's thesis on the speculative fiction of Octavia Butler. I love Butler's stories, and the Afrofuturist heroines she writes into them. They are at once pragmatic and empathetic, the deeply human survivors of mutation, hybridity, and alien genetic intervention, sci-fi predicaments that leave them apart from, or beyond, typical conceptualizations of humanity. They are flawed but powerful, transcending the limits of their species while remaining firmly rooted in their identities as women, as Black, (often) as queer, and equally as likely to head for the stars as they are to time-travel back to the Antebellum South.

Attempting to frame the limitless possibilities of Butler's fiction in academic terms proves plodding, and months of single-minded focus bring me close to burnout. It's through this haze that *Dirty Computer* pierces, reminding me of why I chose to write about Butler, of how much these stories mean to me. I'm in France, writing and visiting family, when I'm woken up by a text from a friend. It's an apology for the time difference, followed by a link to Monáe's recently released video for "Make Me Feel" and the aggressively capitalized assurance that "IT'S GUNNA KILL YOU IN ALL THE RIGHT PLACES." It's an accurate assessment.

The song—made available two months before the release of both *Dirty Computer* and the *Rolling Stone* article in which Monáe first identifies herself as pansexual—is on its own just as good as an official coming out. "Make Me Feel" is a joyous celebration of owning your desire for whatever makes you feel good. Everything from the influence Prince had on the song's production, to the music video extras in their best Bowie, Boy George, and Grace Jones drag, to the ever-present bisexual lighting, is a triumph of subversive self-expression. By the time Tessa Thompson is slowly pushing a popsicle into Monáe's mouth, I am, indeed, killed in all the right places.

"Make Me Feel" and its twin single "Django Jane" sustain me until I am able to appreciate the full spectacle of *Dirty Computer*. A joint album and emotion picture that works as a deeply personal science fictional manifesto for all those who feel undervalued, underserved, and underrepresented, *Dirty Computer* is a blistering polemic still somehow fueled by joy and hope. It's exactly what I need. In 2018, I'm ready to embrace the full range of my queerness. I have a girlfriend, I have community. I have done my thinking, my soul-searching, and am ready to act on this self-knowledge. So, it seems, is Monáe. The evolution of her work and her public persona offers a parallel to my experience that would seem improbably trite if it weren't also true. Both of us now wish to live, if not more authentically, then certainly in a way that is more direct, more deliberate. I wish to live a life that, like the opening lyrics of "Make Me Feel," doesn't need to be spelled out.

And now that I too am in a much more *Dirty Computer*-style mindset, it's especially fascinating to look back on my relationship to *The ArchAndroid*, on the origins of feelings that have now fully come into focus. Speaking with Roxane Gay for *The Cut* in 2020, Monáe says, "I like how my work reveals itself over time. It's like a letter you wrote yourself ten years ago, but when you open it in the future, things start to make sense." I did not understand why *The ArchAndroid* meant so much to me in 2010. I understand in 2018 only with the benefit of hindsight, with the help of the intervening years in which I tried and often failed to find exactly what it was that I wanted out of my relationships, my loves, my life.

Writing this book in 2020, I have yet another perspective, one that looks back on both the hopeful curiosity of 2010 and the joyful arrival of 2018 with new eyes. It's a different world now, in ways that overshadow me completely. I now find myself always worried, always braced for bad news, always ludicrously close to tears. It's likely made my writing far more sentimental than it otherwise might have been, but there is truth in that, I think. My relationship to Cindi's story has changed. I cling to it much more tightly. Writing this book has been difficult but at times strangely cathartic.

There's so much in this world to make me believe that there might not be a future for humanity. Monáe's work offers the chance of a future. Not a perfect one, but one that is possible, one that could, maybe, be waiting for us. If the ArchAndroid can exist in twenty-eighth-century Metropolis and make such a forbidding landscape better, then maybe there's still something to be done in the twenty-first century. Maybe, as Monáe seems to think, we do each have the power to be ArchAndroids, in our own small ways. I've been listening to Monáe's music for a decade, but I find it still contains the same power. Like hooks's angel, *The ArchAndroid* still, after all these years, reminds me of a love that can create worlds, can make possible a future that otherwise seems like it might never arrive. This album has given me many gifts, but hope for the future is the one I might cherish the most.

Acknowledgments

An immense thank you to:

Janelle Monáe and everyone at Wondaland, without whom my life would be far emptier. I hope that, in its small way, this book helps bring your beautiful work to more people.

Chuck Lightning, Wendy Morgan, Kevin Barnes, Chad Weatherford, and Jessee Clarkson for taking the time to speak with me and share their experiences.

Leah Babb-Rosenfeld, Sarah Piña, Rachel Moore, and the entire 33 1/3 and Bloomsbury teams for believing in this book.

Taneasha White, Christian Favreau, and Kelly McDevitt for their invaluable feedback.

My family for their support.

My thesis supervisor Dr. Caroline Brown, for overseeing work that informed this book in many ways.

The Banff Centre for Arts and Creativity and the colleagues I met there.

Octavia E. Butler, who shows me the heart of things.

The Janelle Monáe Fandroids Facebook group, whosampled.com, Guru energy drinks, and Linus D. Cat.

Alison—my ear, my shoulder, my heart.

Also available in the series